Preface by Sir Antony Jay

I do not know why people talk about ma
activity. It is of course two quite distinct activities. managing organisations
and managing projects. This division goes right back to our prehistoric,
indeed pre-human past. The primitive hunting society, a million and more
years ago, needed two separate kinds of management: the long-term
management of the tribe - raising the young, protecting the camp, keeping
order, and the short-term management of the hunting band – locating,
stalking and killing the prey and bringing it safely home. Millions of years
of evolution have imprinted these two instincts deeply embedded in our
genes, and they still control the way we behave in organisations. Every
business, every government department, indeed every institution once it
reaches a size of forty or fifty people, has its people who look after the day-
to-day routines of the camp, and its people who go out and hunt.

What I find odd is that it is the daily routine management that captures
all the attention. Norman Sanders points out that the ratio of management
literature (if that is the right word) is heavily skewed towards the camp,
whereas it is in the hunt, the projects, that you find all the fun, the excitement,
the innovations and above all the growth that keeps organisations alive. It is
projects - successful projects - that are the lifeblood of every organisation.
The problem, for management gurus, is that managing them is an exercise
that is very hard to reduce to rules and routines. Running meetings,
interviewing candidates, appraising staff, writing reports, drawing up cash
flow forecasts, constructing budgets – all these can be taught, and the
rules do not change over the years. But projects, ah, projects, they are a
different matter. They are different, new, chaotic and unpredictable. They
are uncharted waters, beset by the unexpected and the unpredictable.
They change shape as you proceed. No wonder the experts avoid writing
about them.

And yet there are rules. Or, if not hard and fast rules, there are guidelines
and principles and warning lights, and a store of accumulated wisdom. The
trouble is that not a lot of it is written down. There aren't that many people
with the requisite knowledge and experience, and most of them are too
busy with the current project.

That is why this book is so welcome and so important. Norman Sanders
has spent a long working life managing projects and (unlike a lot of
successful project managers) has had that kind of analytical mind that can

i

extract the essential and vital general lessons from a mass of random and apparently unrelated experiences. The result is a book that is the essential bedside companion for everyone involved in the challenging, sometimes frustrating, sometimes rewarding but always surprising world of project management.

Also by Norman Sanders

Stop Wasting Time: Computer-Aided Planning and Control, 1991
Computer-Aided Management: A Manager's Guide to
Profitable Computing, 1985
A Manager's Guide to Profitable Computers, 1979
The St. Merino Solution: A Manager's Guide to Profitable Computing, 1978
The Corporate Computer: How to Live with an Ecological Intrusion, 1973

The Project Manager

Norman Sanders

Cartoons by
Einar Engebretsen

Galleons
Green

Published in 2012 by Galleons Green.
English 1st Edition

Galleons Green Ltd
11 Northgate Street, Ipswich, IP1 3BX, England
#4328, 616 Corporate Way, Suite 2, Valley Cottage, NY 10989-2050 USA
www.galleonsgreen.com

ISBN - paperback format: 9781906960599

A CIP catalogue record for this book is available from the British Library.

Typeset in Proxima Nova by AtriTex Technologies Private Limited
Printed and bound by Lightning Source UK Ltd
Cover Images © Einar Engebretsen

**This book is dedicated to St. Murphy,
the Patron Saint of the Project, and
to some rather more useful colleagues**

IMPOSSIBLE
PR O JECT

**St. MURPHY, The Patron Saint of the Project
... in whose tender care if anything can go wrong
it probably will go wrong**

It wasn't my idea at the start to work on projects. I originally fell amongst the computer folk, few that there were at the time, evolving from doing mathematics on bits of paper, just as computers were in process of being invented. Computers were originally mathematics-only machines, with little superficial resemblance to today's magic devices that everyone else on this planet knows how to use. But to get from the late 1940s to the twenty-first century has taken an untold number of projects, both to move computer technology itself along and to move the application of that technology to the big wide world along with it. So, in company with the ever growing band of brother programmers, who make it all possible, I have been sucked into the world of projects. And with time it has become patently obvious that projects in themselves, independent of their particular details, are beings in their own right. Be they roads, railways, bridges, telephone networks, dictionaries or computer systems, they all share common behavioural patterns, and have created a common language or set of procedures – though no one can be said to have invented them, or claims that they have in any sense been arrived at scientifically. They just came about as part of the job.

It isn't easy after so many years and working with so many people to single out individuals. But there are exceptions and in the Introduction I dwell, in some detail, upon one Grant W. Erwin Jr., my colleague and friend of longest standing. Then there was Gordon Thomson, another leader who led from the front, always working at somebody else's desk, building a brand new agglomeration of hardware and software. He knew intimately what everyone in his team was doing, and was doing a lot of it himself. As did Mike Watts, Simon Powell and Patsy Williams, all of whom are very popular and inspirational leaders. And Dick Eve, who led with quiet modesty, inspiring his people and meeting his deadlines with unassuming nonchalance. Also Ole-Petter Trovaag, who transformed his company's technical sales-support service, unobtrusively into a formidable corporate device. Then there was Richard Nobbs, whom you would never shackle with formal responsibility, but who would be the reality in someone else's organisation, making it all actually work. The list goes on and on. I can't name them all, but I am eternally grateful to all of them.

Then there's Fiona. We all need bouncers, people on whom we can bounce off ideas encapsulated in written sentences, and I have mine in Fiona Powell. I would never let a single utterance out of here without getting the OK from Fiona.

And in addition to these are the people who spawned this book. I would like to thank Piers Venmore-Rowland, my editor, who helped me knock the book into shape. Piers is an erstwhile professor of money and management, a vigorous author of thrillers and general manager of a publishing company. This man now understands project management after piling into the book and understanding the not so subtle differences between the two worlds of management. I wasn't allowed to get away with anything, and his insistence paid off. His comprehension of both worlds led to an expansion of our collective understanding of the nature of management and to subtle additions to the book.

And where would I be without my friend Einar Engebretsen? His cartoons bring to life the prose and give me much pleasure. Thank you Einar.

But no book gets written without the unstinting support of one's family. Anne put up with my daily periods of "playing with the computer" when I should have been helping her with the garden, taking Charlie for a walk and moving the piano. Sorry about that Anne. You are the soul of patience all the time; I'll never do it again! (And the garden has never looked so beautiful.)

About Norman Sanders

Norman is a mathematics and computing graduate from Cambridge University, starting his working life at the very beginning of the computing era. He has worked on many activities at the forefront of computer systems development and the application of computers in the project management process.

This book is the result of decades of continuous experience gained in the world of project management, from the very early days of computers. His experience has been fashioned by workplace projects and a world of problem solving and innovation.

Key activities have included:

Oil pipeline scheduling

The two-thousand mile long Canadian pipeline from Edmonton, Alberta, to Toronto is attached to oil wells and refineries throughout its length. Moreover, it serves as a common carrier for several grades of oil of various degrees of "sweetness", depending on sulphur content. Each refinery is specialised for one particular brand of oil, and cannot accept oil from a wrong source – and every drop must be delivered. This causes very tight scheduling requiring, before the advent of the computer, a scheduling staff of some ten people. This was probably the world's first oil scheduling program, and ran on a very early computer, but it took only four minutes to produce a schedule. But perhaps the most telling value of the system was that it took only four minutes to create a ***reschedule*** in the case of a refinery fire or strike – instead of possibly several days. You can plan time for scheduling, but you can't plan time for rescheduling.

> **You can plan time for scheduling,
> but you can't plan time for rescheduling**

The aircraft industry

The aircraft industry was the first to take serious advantage of the computer, and pioneered much of the use of the computer in the early years of the computer industry. Just about every engineering and commercial problem is to be found in the industry: design, manufacturing, quality control, finance etc, engineering computations, manufacturing work flow, cost accounting, etc. Also keypunching, computer operations, programming training, system planning, implementation and production. Every aircraft was a project in its own right, as were many of its components. And of all of this activity, perhaps the most important and widely applicable to other industries were the invention of Computer-Aided-Manufacturing and Design, and Computer Graphics. This included much computer development and research.

Project planning

The planning of large projects, using the PERT technique, was very time-consuming in the early years, requiring large wall spaces and acres of paper. Moreover, as in most planning situations, **replanning**, something that is always needed, was clumsily difficult. The first attempts at using the computer were certainly promising but were still time-consuming. However, as smaller computers became available, coupled with cleverer higher-level languages and operating systems, it became possible to build a portable, user-friendly device that could be used offshore, onshore, in deserts, in remote rural areas, in trailers, onboard ships and aircraft etc., to plan and replan project activity as it happened. Moreover, we developed planning languages and techniques that became ever easier to learn. In turn, all of this activity led us to understand the dynamics of project work better and to be able to learn and teach project culture to new generations of team workers.

Creating organisations

Creating an organisation is in itself a project. Many of the activities that the author has been involved in have required considerable change to existing organisations and brand new organisations on essentially green-field sites: finding suitable staff, acquiring buildings, structuring organisations, obtaining financial support, determining relationships to other organisations, team-building.

International organisations

Unifying and automating as much as possible the relationships between the headquarters organisation and its subsidiaries. The opportunity for circumventing corporate procedures is proportional to the distance between headquarters and the subsidiary.

Too many projects are based on groundless optimism

The Project Manager

Technological advances are no substitute for common sense

Introduction: The Essence of Project Management

'How shall I start?' he asked himself

The Mad Hatter

The Impossibility of it All

This chapter is intended for anyone concerned with projects; any kind of project, any kind of project worker, at any level, and anyone who has been lucky enough to inherit project genes but is wondering why he is so bored with life. It explains the fundamental problem of projects, setting the scene for the rest of the book.

The problem with projects is that they are logically impossible. Few people realise this and there is a conspiracy of silence amongst those who do. The reason for the latter is that you have to have worked in the project world for some time to realise why things go wrong all the time. However, by that time project work has become your career and you wouldn't want to bite the hand that gave you all that fun. So, despite the impossibility of it all you do it anyway. But, why make your own mistakes? Were they mistakes that have already gone before? Why not spend a bit of time finding out why this was so? This book sets out to help you with this process.

Ah, so I know what I'm about to do, write a book, and I've just started, and I make a note of the date and time.

This book describes the problems and explains why they are essentially intractable. Armed with this knowledge you can set out right from the start each time, creating your own solutions. All managers are different; it's out of bounds for any manager to tell another how to manage (unless they are patently in the wrong job). We can all relate our failures around the campfires of managerial seminars in the hope that others will find better solutions but that's as far as it goes – unless you can divine eternal verities as explanations. An analogy, for the more scientifically inclined: an engineer discovers that π contains an irrational fraction and is therefore never exact, however many digits he uses. He contents himself with an approximation, close enough to prevent his bridge falling down. There are lots of car wheels out there circular enough to keep the cars on the road.

The Two Managerial Worlds

It is not the task of the introduction to list all the essential topics for discussion but one issue does stand out perhaps above all others: it is the essential difference between the project manager and the traditional department manager. Virtually all discussion about management revolves around the latter; it's all about careers, advancement, organisation charts and bonuses. There is a growing number of academic departments running project management degrees. The focus is all too often on management and not the manager. This book provides a valuable insight into the world within which project managers operate.

The Book as a Project

This book is about projects and the problems of managing them. But the book is in itself a project, so it should be a good analogy of any project you care to think about. Well, not quite. Admittedly, it has a beginning. That started a short while ago. Hopefully, it will have a satisfactory end after a spell of life between the two, perhaps the essential properties of any project. However, there is more to some projects than just sitting down and writing. Nevertheless, since this book is the project I'm currently engaged in I'll use it to illustrate this introduction.

Resources

Now all projects require resources of one sort or another. Writing a book is probably the least demanding of resources, so there's not much similarity there. Just one man, his thoughts, a PC and a quiet spot – a far cry from the hurly-burly of industrial projects, especially computer projects.

The Mad Hatter's Quandary

Already in the first paragraph, I have made two startling revelations that you won't find in any of the project management books that have preceded this one. The first is that a project has a beginning but do we know when this beginning was (or will be)? And the second is that at the outset of a project you don't know precisely what you are going to do. Even if you're going to build yet another bridge, the early part of the project is doing the soil mechanics, pertinent only to local conditions, and deciding what type of structure it's going to be, each of which contains, by definition, unknown quantities.

It is true that I know precisely when I started actually writing, but was that really the starting point? Was it not perhaps the decision to do so? Was the thinking process that got me to sit down and write not the actual start? But I wouldn't even have thought of starting had I not already acquired a modicum of experience with projects, so perhaps the project started, even unconsciously, back in the middle of some other project.

> **There is never a clear-cut point at which a project can be said to start**

Or possibly, I had been looking at some old articles that I might have written, or someone else's, and got the germ of the idea. The point that I am making is that there is never a clear-cut point at which a project can be said to start. Out in the real world you have such questions as the budget, the contract, and the decision process to clutter your attempts at clear thinking. Projects do not really start and if you are not decisive they don't end either. They just sort of emerge and having emerged they live for a while and eventually die. When does a book project end? When you've finished doing the writing? When you have finished the corrections that the editor has rudely sent you? At the printers? When the books have arrived at the bookshop or are downloadable as an eBook? When the last one has been pulped? Might there be a second edition requiring your active participation in gathering ideas? A project is enshrouded in a veil of metaphysics, as will be explained in Chapter 1. You must do your best to make some necessarily arbitrary decisions as to the earlier phases of the project, trying to get them agreed to and paid for as best you can.

Shall I start here?

Planning

This book will preach repeatedly about the wisdom of planning and the perils of not doing so. But is this book project planned? No it isn't. At least not in any formal sense. I planned to hide away in a secret barn down in the depths of Somerset to get it going , build up some unstoppable momentum but nothing beyond that. Not yet. I'd rather sketch out an early version to find out whether there was a book there or not. So, as I think of it there is the core of a plan emerging. It consists of tasks to be performed, a list of possible chapter headings, but no dates. But if I were building a bridge, involving people, equipment, time and money, I would have spent this time knocking out the first version of a plan, as explained in Chapters 2 to 6, which I would evolve from day to day throughout its duration and possibly putting it to a multitude of uses as explained in Chapter 14. (Say, how do I know the chapter numbers if I haven't yet written them? Of course, I don't. But I know I'm probably going to write them, and will fill in the numbers at the end. *Don't worry, it's all wrapped up in metaphysics.)*

The book's last sentence: what I hadn't planned was that I would use the secret barn to finish the project as well as start it. I predicted each day, right to the end, that I had just one day to go – day after day. The deadline was breathing down my neck. So it was time to leave Somerset and move the project on the path to completion.

The Organisation

At the moment no one cares whether I get this project going or not, except me. But if you're building a bridge a lot of people will be breathing down your neck from day one (whichever day that might be), and you will be expecting a lot of help from them as it grows and takes on a life of its own. You'll need to know from the start what sort of organisation you're doing this for. Do they understand what projects are all about? The differences between projects and organisational structures? Between the nature of project people and staff people? Do you know who your boss is? Or how many bosses you're likely to have at one time? To get the help you need are you going to have to wander the corridors, cap in hand, or do they already have a project office staffed with friendly faces? All this is described in Chapters 15, 16 and 17.

But Don't Abandon Hope

And finally, though really initially, you must be very careful what you are doing. Are you agreeing to something well defined? Do those around you understand what they are asking you to do?

> ### This is a "How to Think About It" and not a "Do It My Way" book

Is there any reason to doubt its viability? Who really believes in it? And about another ninety five questions to help you defend yourself against the slings and arrows. All this is described in Chapter 7, which you should perhaps read before you read its predecessors. It may put you off and decide you against any further thought. But be not afraid, this is not a *Do It My Way* book. That would be most boring. Rather, it is a *How To Think About It* book, relying on the unique you to get it right your way. Furthermore, although the book has been arranged with the rudiments of logical structure, you can read the chapters in more or less any order in which serendipity leads you. All I've done really is write down key thoughts about projects culled from a lifetime of watching other people do them and trying to do them myself, in the hope that they will get you thinking.

The Personal Computer

Underlying almost everything discussed in the book is the computer. There was little use made of the computer in the project world before about 1970, but in the decade up to 1980, as computers began to shrink in terms of the amount of space they occupied and began to move up from the floor onto the desk en route to the lap, they began to emerge as an ever more useful component of the project manager's toolbox. With today's PC, attached, as it is, to a rapidly developing global network of hard and soft components, it has become central to everything the project needs and does. It appears in every chapter of this book. Although the reader may not be a computer expert, he will undoubtedly be deeply familiar with the standard functions supplied by the computer industry and would not imagine doing anything in the old-fashioned way. The downside of all this is that I may not be entirely alone in feeling that one of the triumphs of the personal computer has been the empowerment of the personal assistant (the old-fashioned secretary). You'll have to make your own coffee now.

**One of the triumphs of the personal computer
has been the empowerment of the Personal Assistant**

The Manager

There seems to be no profession called project management, though there certainly are books on the subject, this being yet another one, all presumably based on practical experience. For myself I have learnt a lot, much of it by making mistakes, but mostly by watching others bring about miracles of creation. And I should say right away that, as in all walks of life and work, there are enormous differences between people's ability to work in teams, but I was lucky enough to bump into the world's best right at the outset. I joined the Boeing Company in 1959, where already computers were being used to make things out of aluminium, as opposed to printing numbers on paper, and one of the first people I met in America was Grant W. Erwin Jr, probably the best project manager on this planet. We were to enjoy a long partnership in which I watched in pure astonishment at the way he ran groups of people to get things done.

Grant's project history is a unique one. His first was to get into the war ahead of the United States, volunteering as a navigator in the Royal Canadian Air Force en route to the Royal Air Force in Britain, thence to the U.S. Army Air Force in B24 bombers in India. Each sortie was in itself a project – not least the final two. In the first of these he was the only crew member still both alive and conscious – and he was not a pilot. But he had watched pilots doing their job and he found an airfield and landed a giant aircraft for the first (and last) time. In his last operation he was the sole survivor and was thrown into his next project, surviving life as a guest of the Emperor of Japan.

Back in civilian life Grant joined Boeing and became one of the stalwarts of the company's drive to move the general public around the planet safely and cheaply. Grant was a mathematician and the way he did it was via the computer. In those days Boeing led the world in the use of computers but computing is mostly about people. We were pioneering a brand new technology, and it was natural that the initiative came from the lower deck, not from senior management. And the greatest of these initiatives was what was to become known as Computer-Aided Design (CAD). We had the great good fortune to be allowed by the management of the 727 airplane to convert its design intent into a mathematical definition, which we could use to draw lines and cut parts, all under the control of the computer. Today CAD is a tried and trusted technology used throughout the world, but at the start of the 727 it was just a gleam in a few eyes and a collection of untried computer programs; it had never been attempted, therefore the programs had never been tested. But they let us do it. They entrusted us to build the

727 airplane using untried technology, and whenever I think of it my blood runs cold. The only chance of success it had was that Grant was running it. No one else could have done it. I don't suppose he gave CAD a second thought. And he did it because he was a through and through born project manager. That is to say, he was a **leader**; he led from the front. He knew what everyone was doing. He had the necessary popularity amongst his team. No one complained of late night and weekend working. He knew his way around both the engineering and manufacturing departments. He knew the mathematics, and what didn't already exist he invented. Where do I stop? He had everything I write about in this book.

So, thanks Grant. You've inspired, by now, generations of us, though you'll never admit it. This book is wrapped around you.

The Project Owner

Is it clear to whom the project manager reports? Who is the occupant of the hot seat in charge of the whole project? Is it a person or a committee? In the case of the public sector has anyone taken ultimate responsibility and will they be there for the life of the project?

The project owner is at the very least the budget holder and the champion of the project. Sadly, all too often the role of the project owner is overlooked in the management of projects. Such an omission is fraught with danger.

Computer-based Planning Systems

As time has gone on, computer users have moved physically further and further away from the computer programmer. Right at the start we had to write the programs ourselves, spending much time in the computer room dropping punched cards on the floor; there was simply no one else to do it. But in parallel with the evolution of hardware, a software industry has evolved. Today when we discuss computers, decide what functions we need, etc., our attention is concentrated almost entirely on the software, and now this planet abounds with people who are expert at Word, Excel and PowerPoint, and in our industry the likes of Microsoft Project. But very few users know anything at all about the workings of the software. Indeed, the software technology is getting ever more remote from the user, and could be on another continent or even somewhere on the moon. The user simply doesn't need to know.

In particular, the computer software of primary importance to the project planner and user comes in many varieties as a range of providers has evolved since the 1970s. Project planning systems are all slightly different in appearance on the screen, and differ somewhat in particular components, but at heart they are all identical, as described in Chapter 3. And from time to time I have used a particular system in the book, Microsoft Project (MSP), to help illustrate the discussion. It has the advantage of being widespread. It is probably the most well known system. However, it may not be the best for your corporate purposes, though it is satisfactory for my illustrative purposes.

And the Book's Audience

Who ought to be reading this book? Well there is an immediate array of people closely coupled to the project culture, primarily the project manager, the project owner, the occupant of the hot seat in charge of the whole thing, who lives with it day and night and upon whose desk every buck stops. This book is primarily his or hers – but far from solely. Throughout the book "he" will be used and not he or she. In my experience, women make excellent project managers and are sadly under-represented in the industry. At one step above the project manager will be the project owner, or sponsor, the corporate champion of the project; he who understands and represents the project at the stratospherical level (see Chapter 8). He will probably be the originator of the project, the budget-getter and probably the customer-calmer.

The owner needs to be fully conversant with the physical nature of the project, the contract that gives the project life, the order of magnitude of its cost, and the latest estimates of the project duration. But, he will almost certainly not get into the diabolical details of its implementation. Though not all chapters will be of absorbing interest, the owner should nevertheless know what they contain. As the owner, he will inevitably be in close contact with the project manager to seek specific detail, when required, and will be able to use these chapters to gain simple background explanations of the main strands of project flow.

Central to all project activity is the need for planning and one of the key members of the project team is the planner, about whom much will be said. The planner could well also be the project manager. Certainly this will be the case with small projects. However, planning isn't just a one-time occupation, especially in larger projects. In all probability the total time reworking a plan, resulting from the cruel buffeting of unanticipated reality, will exceed the time spent creating the initial version by the time the project comes to its welcome end. But even if the project manager doesn't create the plan, he will be very close at hand as it is evolved and will work intimately with it throughout its useful life.

Then there are the human resources, the toilers, the people who do the work. They should at the very least know how a plan is made, and it wouldn't hurt if they actually planned their own activities, meshing them in with the total version. They should find the discussion of planning of interest, leading on to specific detail provided with the company planning system. Furthermore, if they feel themselves to be of the project persuasion in corporate life, rather than of the traditional managerial, they might find the book useful in giving them clues to a managerial career.

Since most projects have a clearly understood customer to satisfy, external or internal, it would be very helpful if the customer were also able to read and understand a plan.

> ## The client won't get rich on penalty clauses

This is not to spy on their supplier but to aid the information process between the warring camps. I have not infrequently been in a customer confrontation in which I have had to make it clear that in reality we are a single team. Neither side gains from an error on the part of the other; the client won't get rich on penalty clauses. A savvy customer will want to include the plan in the contract – and see clearly where the contractual items appear in the plan. This discussion is taken up in Chapter 7.

In Chapter 10 we mention the back office: the company lawyer and the internal mail deliverer. Although they may not find themselves by name involved in the plan, they should nevertheless be well aware of the goings-on in the project. The project is the engine room of the organisation: it pays their wages, and this book gives them a better than cursory impression of how it's done.

Then finally we have the Head Shed, the Headquarters or Command Post. I suppose much of the need for this book is that most organisations are populated by folk of two water-tight cultures, if the ghost of C. P. Snow[1] will allow. You may find a modicum of ad nauseam here and there whenever the discussion of project versus staff raises its head. Nevertheless, few organisations contain stratospheric people who know what PERT is. PERT?! Read on, band of bonus brothers, we are all in this together.

But each chapter carries a target list of readers in the first paragraph.

Collecting Experience

What interests me as I finish this introduction is how much it cost me. Of course, there's no money to be made from it. Not yet, anyway. No one has asked me to write it, so there's no one to bill. And I haven't spent any money, other than the price of a modicum of ink and that of a scrap of paper. And it is often that way. Indeed, a lot of project effort goes unreported and unrewarded; people feel that if work isn't directly billable it needn't be recorded. The trouble is that in this way valuable experience is lost, experience you'd like to have next time you find yourself estimating a similar project. Thus every hour expended on a project should be recorded, whether or not it's reported to the costing system. We'll expand on this later in the book.

The Book's Structure

The manifold components of any discussion of the nature of projects make it difficult to treat it in a linear way; you are forced somehow to make reference to features that you have not yet introduced. This book is non-linear, it isn't a novel. There is therefore inevitable need for cross-referencing between chapters. I have tried to keep this to a minimum, consistent with clarity. For example, the discussion of language emerges in six of the chapters, and the Duke of Wellington in three. (Hey, what's the dear old Duke doing in the world of projects? It is he who invented project management, his main technology being his horse.)

Bring On The Cartoonist

You will notice that the pages of this book are graced with cartoons. These are here to reinforce a point. They are serious business. Each one is an illustration of the human condition, in particular as found in the field of

---

1   Charles Percy Snow was an English chemist and writer who served in several important positions in the Civil Service and publicly lamented the gulf between scientists and literary intellectuals.

industrial endeavour. Einar and I hope you recognise and agree with most of them and find them pertinent to the subject matter. We feel that a good cartoon is worth many paragraphs of prose and Einar has that rare and magic quality that enables him to convert a loose and even abstract idea into instantaneous and tangible form. So, if you don't have time to read, just look at the pictures.

An image is worth a thousand words

The next chapter ...

... describes the metaphysical nature of the emergence of a project. Later in the book we liken it unto the creation of the universe, but at this stage we content ourselves with throwing out the challenge of how to cope with two irreconcilable ideas: that at the outset the project must precede its manager while, equally, the manager must precede the project. The rest of the book discusses how to cope with this logical impasse.

Chapter 1: The Metaphysics of Project Initiation

I've started so I'll finish

Magnus Magnusson

In the Beginning: Gathering Scattered Rosebuds

In the first paragraph of the Introduction, I blithely stated that the project of writing started a short while ago. I knew precisely when it started; I noted the exact time of day. All projects are like this; they start somewhere at some point in time. Work starts, resources start to be consumed, money begins to flow, time begins to be expended, deadlines begin to die, and the whole catastrophe rears its head from the primeval corporate swamp. At least that is what seems to happen.

However, reality is somewhat different. I know exactly when I started doing the typing, and I can say that that's when the official project started. But was that the start of the true project? I couldn't write this book without having lived through many years of projects. I needed something to write about. It had to be non-fiction. It had to be worth reading. It needed a purpose: that of trying to help people at all stages of their careers. It ought to be the book I would have liked to have read decades ago. But it would be utterly artificial to claim that this project started then. So when did it start?

> **The whole catastrophe rears its head from the primeval corporate swamp**

Well, I was trying to get up a mountain a week ago, buffeted by some rather violent winds which prevented my achieving my goal. It was yet another failed project. By now, I thought, I have failed so many projects that I ought to have learnt enough to get it right every time. Moreover, I should be able to pass on the fruits of this learning to others less fortunate than me who have not yet met so much failure.

I had already written a number of books and articles over the years, extolling the virtues of good planning, determined management, team-building, budget-watching, the linguistic problem, and staying off the company organisation chart, but articles get buried in the graveyard of time. Better to do some disinterment, start again, and create something more holistic.

Articles get buried in the graveyard of time

So, sitting behind a rock in a forlorn attempt to eat a wind-swept sandwich I fished into my pocket and found a scrap of Rolo wrapper upon which I made a few notes. So that's when it started. At the three thousand foot level on a windy Sunday, a week before the calm of a garden shed at the ten foot level in Suffolk, or the secret barn down in Somerset. But was it the actual writing or the decision to write, or the thought that led to the decision? An infinite telescope of questions.

I made a few notes. So that's when it started

Big time projects are even worse to handle. Though you might think that this is all about angels on pinheads it isn't. Most projects are conceived on the back seat of the organisation, resulting in unclear statements of purpose, superficial specifications, inadequate estimates of requirements, unhappy team assignments, messy accounting, poor establishment of accountability and profitability - and an obituary in Private Eye.

I shall initiate this book with a chapter about project initiation, a topic rarely discussed and only vaguely understood. But it is an essential component of getting it right. So please read on. By the time you reach Chapter 7 – which is about the Project Initiation Checklist – the concept should be clearer. The whole thing is a sandwich. I hope it tastes OK.

How to Get to Day Zero

Project initiation is the process of taking the project from some misty something through to Day Zero – the first action day. The project initiation phase consists in turn of a series of minor phases as ideas become clearer and costs mount. Is each of these steps, though, part of the project? People are working and being paid. Somehow, they are justifying the money, so someone is paying them, and presumably backing the idea.

Or are these steps regarded as preceding the project? And who decides what each step shall consist of and whether there shall be a next? Indeed, are these steps formally recognised or are they a sort of misty series of unclear attempts to do something? If so, at what point should the mist clear? And just because the ideas are hardening should they inevitably lead to a project? Lots of questions, so let's explore them in a little detail.

> ## Most new ideas come while wallowing in the bath

Enter Wittgenstein

Most new ideas come while wallowing in the bath. You feel good. Your thought processes are not interrupted. You play with duck and boat. Then suddenly you get this fantastic idea: a sun-powered mouse trap, a piece of software that links the exercise bike to Google Maps, a button-free microwave, a non-digital watch. Eureka! You grab your mobile phone. Gotta check with old Fred. He's the world champion at knocking down new ideas. We hate him, but he saves us every time from our own best of intentions. But someone else is now involved. Has a project started? Is the idea contained in the project? Or does the idea precede the project? Deep stuff this. Come back Wittgenstein.

Other projects start with lunch: salesman and prospective customer wrapped in a fog of serendipity. There's no one around who actually knows what he's talking about, but something's started. And as soon as the prospect is out of earshot the salesman grabs his phone. But who pays for the lunch? Does it come out of the project budget? What project budget? What budget? What project?

Then there's the boardroom version. (Avoid these like the plague!) The chairman invites any objections to his proposed Patagonia Banana Project. He knows how long it will take, how much it will cost, and the eventual business it will create. But how does he know all this? Obviously, a lot of money has already been expended. Did the project actually start a couple of years ago? Is this another bath project further downstream, or further down the plughole? Where has the money come from? Will it show up in the project accounts?

But What Will it Cost?

One way or another, having spawned the project, now consider its economics. What might it cost in terms of manpower, equipment, materials, workplaces, finance, and so on? Well, what does it entail? You can't answer any of these questions until you have a fairly detailed plan. Now there are two ways of obtaining a plan: either the project is sufficiently similar to a predecessor and by sheer luck, someone has preserved its history. Alternatively, somebody has to sit down and think it through using a computer planning system. The former method, while much more accurate, will have the problem of pure disbelief. It is likely to show the project will cost far too much and that the new project should be dropped (which is the best thing to do with most projects anyway). Or the actual times and costs will need to be reduced to something the company thinks it can afford in the hope that next time around it can do it better (though we seldom do). The latter is a recipe for disaster, of course.

However, if the project is an entirely new one, and someone has to plan it, who is going to do the planning? And who is going to check that the computer-generated planning system is an accurate portrayal of what will be required. I'll return to this question in just a moment.

More Wittgenstein

At some point we will have to appoint a project manager: someone who is going to live with it night and day until it is accepted by its customer. But when is this? At what point during the emergence of the project do we sanctify it with a manager? After the project has started or before? Which comes first? Can a project be said to exist before it has a manager? Usually the manager will not have invented the project nor discovered the need for it. He is usually appointed after someone else has proposed it. So, *ipso facto*, the project has to precede its manager. However, a potential manager would be foolish to accept the job without the opportunity of understanding and influencing it.

The project has to precede its manager

Since most projects start out as fairly wild, optimistic and woolly ideas, the hoped-for elapsed times and costs will usually be hopelessly optimistic. If the person with the responsibility for seeing it through accepts the estimates (if you can call them that) without subjecting them to some critical examination, including the first version of the plan, they are heading for trouble. So if you allow the manager-elect to influence it he is almost certain to change it – even to the extent of convincing you that the project isn't viable. So the manager has to precede the project! It can't really be said to exist until a project manager salutes it smartly and agrees to carry it out. Come back yet again Wittgenstein.

So the manager has to precede the project!

So where has all this got you? It is at this point at which we really understand that the existence of a project is all bound up with metaphysics, as I said in the Introduction.

To complicate matters even more we must ask the next question. We have already asked whether the idea is encapsulated in the project or not. Also whether or not its manager is encapsulated in the project.

Now we have to ask whether a project can exist before it has a budget? You would be foolhardy to give the go-ahead before you had a solid estimate of the potential cost and a guaranteed source of finance. So the budget precedes the project; it is part of the decision process. But it costs money to secure these things, as well as a competent planner with a personal stake in its success. The best person to do this planning is clearly the project manager himself; otherwise, as we have just said, it might have to be redone. And since you can't have a project manager without an identified project to manage, the project must precede the budget. So we have two intertwined veins of metaphysics. Sort that one out Wittgenstein!

A Surfeit of Perceptions

Beyond that, there may be more than one perception of what the project is all about. There were at least three perceptions of the Sydney Opera House project. (It cost, as you will remember, seventeen times the original estimate.) It was the creation of a place in which to listen to people singing; it was iconic. It was the beautification of the Sydney skyline, and it was a monument to the architect.

Somehow, all this preliminary activity has to be brought to a close and the project is started (or the decision is made to abandon it). Day Zero has to be named. How you do this is also the subject of a separate discussion. Suffice it for the moment to realise that the birth of a project is enshrouded in inevitable philosophical mist, and unless each step is carried out with a maximum of available clarity the only advice to those about to embark on a project is – "don't!". You may be about to mortgage your shirt.

However, for British projects there may be one exception, the Machiavellian financiers of PFI projects. If it is big enough and its importance perceived to be great enough, you might be able to get it accepted as a Private Finance Initiative (PFI) and have some government department guarantee it, and its cost escalator clauses, for several decades, with a bundle of taxpayers' money.

**The birth of a project is enshrouded in
inevitable philosophical mist**

To help you determine whether or not to accept an offer to manage a project you may turn to Chapter 7, which contains many questions to help you make your mind up. If you know of any question that I have omitted, please don't keep it to yourself. I can't be expected to think of everything.

The next chapter ...

... is concerned with creating a numerical structure with which to represent the item to be delivered by the project. Although this structure is called a "Work Breakdown Structure" (WBS), it has nothing directly to do with work. It has all to do with the finished article, once the work has been done. The work involved is described in Chapter 3 and following chapters. WBS is an unfortunate term, but it has been around for years and there's little we can do about it except to explain it.

Chapter 2: Breakdown Structures – The Anatomy of a Plan

I have a cunning plan

Baldrick

Lead up to Day Zero

The detail of this chapter should be of primary interest to project managers and planners. The main concern of project owners, and those to whom they report, lies in the knowledge that they have a system that works.

As the previous chapters have clearly stated, it isn't always obvious when a project can be claimed to have started. A start date needs some pontification from the higher echelons of the organisation. But what needs to be done to convince that person that the time has come to pontificate? The thing to be done is to run a pre-project, a spontaneous symphony of events, the heat of which might well exceed the light. The pre-project forms the essence of Chapter 9, Coping with the Run Up. During the inevitable run-up to the start date a lot of healthy activity will have been engaged in: customer-salesman lunches, salesman-engineer meetings, computer modelling, rough sketching, detailed drawing, physical model making, e-mailing and a lot of shouting and even fisticuffs, both verbal and physical. The possible detail will take many forms depending on the nature of the beast, be it a sales brochure, a boutique or a bridge. The brochure will require a mock-up of some sort, the boutique will need a variety of drawings, while the bridge might need some soil mechanical investigation as well as a model competition.

In each case the company's corridors will get knee-deep in discarded ideas. However, there is one thing that should not be discarded, the cost of it all. But that isn't easy to quantify because before somebody has set up a budget the money will of necessity come from a variety of sources: the sales department, the drawing office, the workshop, computing and the travel budget. You ought to have a system to account for the contributions, to be added eventually to the cost of the project, to make the whole thing ship-shape; but that isn't easy. This pre-project is impossible to plan; it is more like an anthill than a racehorse; it doesn't have a number on its back to charge to. But at some stage this activity will either run out of steam and die a natural death or someone will call a halt, sprinkle some holy water and declare that it has become a project in its own right. Tomorrow, Day Zero, we start and Fred has been appointed project manager. Read on...

Day Zero

You have reached the day, by whatever route, on which it has been decided upon high to invest serious company money in subjecting the nascent project to a phase of detailed planning. There has been a surfeit of planning during the build-up to today; much of it oral, not all of it in entirely sober circumstances, but some of it actually written down, and even accompanied by calculations. However, each document, model, calculation, etc. has been stamped with adjectives such as preliminary, unofficial, not to be taken seriously and don't touch. But someone has decided that, for whatever reason, it is time we produced some solid timings and costs – and some pictures of what it might really look like.

However, even at this stage it could turn out to be a no-hoper. In this life, most of what we categorise as preliminary eventually dies as unviable, and it is far cheaper and meritorious to spend money trying to draw it, model it and plan it than actually creating it before you know what it is you ought to be creating. Money spent preventing the company going broke is by definition a good investment. On the other hand, you might well be lucky and be able to demonstrate a modicum of feasibility.

This chapter describes how to start the process by drawing a diagram of the structure to be created for the project (aircraft, pipeline, rail network, etc.). It should be of interest to a small group of people at the managerial-technical interface; in addition to the project manager, the project owner, the project customer and detail people at the next layer down.

Breakdown Structures

In order to plan the production of any object, from the smallest component to the complete edifice, we need to create a picture of the structure showing its progressive assembly into larger and fewer components, ending up with the object itself. The edifice can be anything. It is a new product, or service, that the project sets out to achieve. It can be a motor car, aircraft, washing machine or offshore platform, or it can be an annual sales brochure, computer program or a ticketing system. Whatever the object, it will always consist of components, which will in turn consist of subcomponents, and so on down to the nuts and bolts, grande jettés, chapters and paragraphs.

Such a picture is called a **Product Breakdown Structure**, and we create it by disassembling it progressively from the whole right down to its basic elements. A bicycle, for example, consists of a frame, wheels, mudguards, handlebars, saddle, driving function, gearing and brakes. A wheel, in turn, consists of a tyre, rim, hub, spokes, ball bearings and nuts, while the driving function consists of pedals, cranks, hub, front cogwheels, chain and rear cogwheels. And so on. The weight of the bike is the sum of the weights of its component parts – not forgetting the paint.

The Product Breakdown Structure, then, shows the physical parts of the whole, grouped in a logical and pictorial way.

What it does not show, however, is the work needed to be done to carry out the assembly: attaching the brake cables to the handlebars, putting the handlebars on the frame, and so on. The Product Breakdown Structure in isolation does not tell us how to build the bicycle, how long it will take or how much it will cost – the cost being the sum of the prices of the components plus the costs of assembling them.

> **The weight of the bike is the sum of the weights of its component parts – not forgetting the paint**

We need then to draw another picture, identical in form to the Product Breakdown Structure, which we could call the Process Breakdown Structure. To each element of the former there is a corresponding element of the latter. The former contains such information as material codes, prices and weights, while the latter contains the times and costs of doing the work.

The two together constitute a picture which is commonly known as the Work Breakdown Structure (WBS). This is an unfortunate term because, of course, it represents more than simply the work. But it has become firmly established in the vocabulary, and is unlikely to disappear.

A WBS then is an analysis of the whole in terms of its parts in a nice orderly way. It starts at the top as a single entity and it finishes at the bottom at a level of detail comprising perhaps thousands of entities. The trick is to analyse down to a sensible level, a level that provides a satisfactory basis for planning the work PERT, as explained in Chapter 3. As a more realistic illustration, let us take the example of an offshore oil and gas platform.

The entity is the entire platform, an object consisting of a deck, and all that that entails, and its support. Let us identify these numerically as 1 and 2 respectively. Let us further analyse the deck, component code 1. The deck consists of a number of major modules, which we could number as follows...

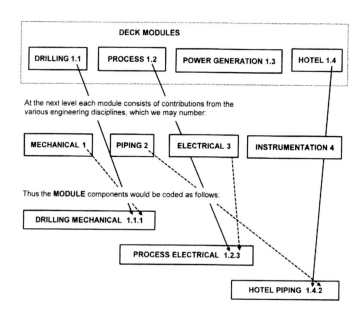

A Work Breakdown Structure

And so on, each component number taken from the lists above. Thus, the first three levels of the WBS are fairly straightforward. Beyond this, at level 4, the possibilities begin to spread out. It could continue to be physical items, pumps, generators and lifts, or it could be reporting time-periods (months, say) cost-of-work-containers. Thus DRILLING module, mechanical cost, month 1 would be 1.1.1.1, while the PROCESS module, electrical cost, month 6 would be 1.2.3.6.

Alternatively, level 4 might represent packages of work contracted out to the suppliers.

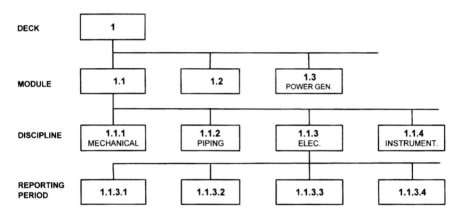

A Pictorial Representation of a Work Breakdown Structure

Here you see the deck consisting of the drilling function, the process function, the hotel, etc. At the next level, you see the drilling function consisting of the mechanical component, the piping, the electro, instrumentation, etc. Let us say that the fourth level is the reporting level. Here, as an example, we have shown the electro function reporting each month.

Clearly, the picture is really multi-dimensional and the number of boxes multiplies up to something quite large, depending on reporting requirements; each WBS is unique. There are general principles, practices and standards, such as drawing numbers and part numbers; however similar to its predecessors, each structure is the result of a new design and the injection of the results of new experience as we learn how to do it better.

Thus, a WBS is a special way of representing a physical thing. At the working level each element is represented by drawings, material codes, parts lists, etc, and is accompanied by the cost to date of creating it. The WBS has, in itself, nothing to do with time. It says nothing about the actions that have to be carried out, how long they should take or who should do them, and so on. This is the province of the PERT chart, a structure for planning the work, the subject of the following chapters.

To take the WBS to its logical conclusion, why not depict it on the computer screen as a picture of the actual product of the project, rather than as a code? If the object is a bridge, why not depict the WBS as a bridge and all its parts? Then, by clicking on hotspots on the picture we could step our way down the WBS, depicting each level as a detailed drawing of that level. This idea has been around for some time, but its implementation is not easy and if one is not very careful components can get lost. Nevertheless, the company, PCF Ltd (pcfltd.co.uk), has done just this.[2]

The important question right now, however, is how to connect the two; how to dovetail the WBS level with its PERT time component? This is explained in Chapter 6.

> ## If you feel a little adventurous, build yourself a hospital

While the WBS provides a logical basis for creating the PERT chart, an integrated coding scheme between the two provides the basis for cost reporting. Indeed, on the way down, a WBS is a physical description mechanism while on the way up it is a cost-accounting mechanism.

As we saw above, a further function of the WBS is that the numbering arrangement enables it to be juggled to provide more or less any view that a person needs; it can be transposed.

---

[2] See Chapter 17.

As an illustration of transposition, let us use a different example. Suppose a builder has three projects on the go, the Central Hospital (WBS code 1..), the Station Extension (2..) and the Togetherness Apartments(3..) The WBS coding could be as follows:-

	Central Hospital 1..		Station Extension 2..			Togetherness Apartments 3..	
Level 1							
Level 2	Site Prep. .1.	F'dations .2.	Walls .3.	Floors .4.	Roofs .5.	Finish .6.	Inspection .7.
Level 3	Excavation ..1	Concrete ..2	Bricklaying ..3	Carpentry ..4	Glazing ..5	Plumbing ..6	Electrical ..7

An Example of a Work Breakdown Structure Coding

Thus Central Hospital, Walls Carpentry would be 1.3.4, while Station Extension, Finish Plumbing would be 2.6.6.

This is the project manager's view of the structural breakdown of a project, enabling costs to be appropriately summarised up to the project level. However, the chief bricklayer has a very different view of things. To him, bricklaying goes at the top, while the particular project his brickies are currently working on goes at the bottom; the levels structure is up-side-down. To create the chief bricklayer's view of the world we simply swap position 1 with position 3 in the coding to get the following typical picture:-

	Bricklaying 3..					
Level 1						
Level 2	Foundations 32.			Walls 33.		
Level 3	Central Hospital 321	Station Extension 322	T'therness Apartments 323	Central Hospital 331	Station Extension 332	T'therness Apartments 333

The Chief Bricklayer's View of the WBS

In this view costs are collected on site and summarised up to the trade level. This allows the chief bricklayer to be responsible for the costs incurred in bricklaying, providing him with an initial budget per project and a mechanism for comparing actual expenditures with budgets during the life of each project.

This transposition of WBS coding reflects the matrix organisation of the people involved, with a specified team responsibility for each project, but with trade departments, or possibly subcontractors, responsible for carrying out the work packages.

This completes the introduction to breakdown structures but before continuing why not draw a few of your own to make sure you understand the ideas? Try something easy like building a toboggan, or if you feel a little adventurous build yourself a hospital.

The next chapter ...

... is one of the most important in the book; organising the work required to create the components of the WBS. Project initiation. PERT. Network analysis. Critical Path. Resources beyond time.

Chapter 3: Organising the Work

Work is the curse of the drinking classes

Oscar Wilde

Introduction

This chapter is aimed at project planners and managers. It isn't easy to avoid explaining confusing (though perhaps simple) calculations, especially backwards time. So this chapter might not be much fun for people who left their maths classroom some years ago. And most project managers and planners probably know the stuff already. However this is how it works and if you have a better way of explaining it do please send it to me. The main point is that it works, it is invaluable and that all planning systems should give you the same dates.

We have agreed, perhaps at long last, to the Work Breakdown Structure (WBS), and we now have to make a plan as to how the project will be carried out. The first, fundamental step in this process is that of dealing with time. What are the tasks required by each of the WBS components and how long should they take? The goal is to define the structure of an implementation, an assemblage of people, materials, equipment, facilities – and time, etc. to do the work to produce the bridge, the pipeline, the factory, the telephone system or the guide book, whatever the project may be.

The Target Audience

This chapter is intended for senior managers with a stake in the project but little, if any, practical involvement in the detail; they are in the layer immediately above that of the project manager.

However, the project manager and his subordinates should look at this chapter as being an introduction to Chapter 5, which deals in detail with the topic of planning resources other than time.

This chapter sets out to solve the problem of the communication between the project team and the managerial/customer structure to which the project reports. In practice this communication process is bandied about by pictures of what is going on – as opposed to what was promised – accompanied by written narrative (you hope), oral narrative, arm-waving and a modicum of vituperation.

There will still be misunderstandings

This chapter won't get you all the way because the pictures (diagrams, graphs, flowcharts, etc.) aren't of the project itself but of the information embedded in the project plan. There will still be sources of misunderstanding, but if you get the hang of this chapter you will be close to minimising them. As you read this chapter try to put yourself in the shoes of the project manager explaining it all to your board chairman.

A Little of the Fundamental Jargon

So the project manager has decided that the project they've landed him with is viable. Or he's throwing caution to the winds. Either way the first thing for him to do is to create the plan with which the project is going to live throughout its duration. If the run up, the initiation process, has been done reasonably well there should already be a semblance of a plan, a coarse version, which ought to lead the project manager to the fine-mesh version. At least it should tell him who has been involved so far; people he can interrogate.

Change is the essence of planning

Project Initiation

We stated right at the start of the book that from the standpoint of pure logic, projects couldn't start. Well that might be OK in theory, but if we want to get that bridge built we'd better get it started. So, armed with the Project Initiation document (PI), described in Chapter 7, the project manager sets about creating a plan of some considerable detail, documented in an easy to change format. Change is the essence of planning because the detail garnered during the early phases will inevitably act as a signpost and teach all concerned much about the project that had been hitherto hidden, as we shall see later.

This means that you can't avoid using the computer; change happens quickly and sabotages the pretty pictures you started out with. There is an abundance of computer-based project planning systems available. They vary greatly in appearance and range of features, but at their core they are all similar; you will get the same dates as you run the plan, whichever system you use. It is therefore important to understand how this core works.

The following describes the components of these planning systems and seeks to make them as accessible as possible, introducing long-standing terminology, now accepted by most practitioners. It is all about something called PERT charts, where PERT originally stood for Polaris Evaluation and Review Technique, though today the P stands for Project.

Project planning consists of arranging a galaxy of tasks, each more or less an indivisible component of the project; do this, do that, do some other thing, in some sort of logical order, each bearing a description of the work to be done, who shall do it, with what resources, where, in how much time and so on. It sounds simple, and, at the elemental level, it is something like the cells of the body. And, as with cells, a task contains many elements and is itself contained as an element in an even larger structure. But, as with the human body, as cell is added to cell the entity starts to get quite complicated. And with complication it is vital to know that the cells themselves work, as well as the logic connecting them.

Extensions to the Core System

This chapter is about the core of planning, the building blocks enabling you to create plans with as much complexity as is needed. However, as we shall see in later chapters, since every company is different there is a wide range of features not included in the basic system supplied by the software industry and a very active industry of software suppliers ready to supply bespoke software add-ons to suit your needs.

The Elements of a Network or PERT chart

The basis of any project plan, then, is a network of task names or descriptions. But, just to warn you, the trade abounds with alternative words for network: logic diagram, precedence diagram, activity on node diagram, to name some. However, the most definitive and time-tested term is PERT chart.

A task may be any self-contained and coherent element of the total work to be carried out during the life of the project, e.g. DIG TRENCH, LAY PIPE, MIX CONCRETE, POUR CONCRETE, ALLOW TO DRY. This all sounds straightforward enough. It goes on all the time out there in the workaday world. But behind each pretty obvious Task Name there lies a whole slew of supporting characters, and primarily there needs to be an estimate of the elapsed time required to carry it out, the Duration (coded DU). To estimate the time taken to dig the ditch you need to know what lies concealed beneath the grass: is it clay, pebbles, rock, an unsuspected utility pipe or a Roman wall? Ditches take far longer to dig in rocky Sweden than they do in soil-laden Denmark (somebody has already had to do some soil surveying). That in itself can have been an element in a previous project, a feasibility study perhaps to determine whether the soil conditions could support the skyscraper.

EINAR

Nobody's looking

Within the plan there will have been the task ORDER PIPING –
early enough to get it there on time. If not there will be avoidable
delays and cries of "Hey, and where's Charlie's wheelbarrow?" can
be avoided.

Just writing down the names of the tasks brings up a whole plethora of
activities – all of which need to be included in the plan; remove a task at
your peril! Alternatively, add one and become a folk hero.

What's Charlie's wheelbarrow doing here?

Task Relationships

So at the very core of a task is its name and duration. But between the
tasks we have to specify their relationships. In this simple example it's
pretty obvious that we have to dig the trench before we can lay the pipe,
a relationship we can specify in the following way, each description in a
tidy box:-

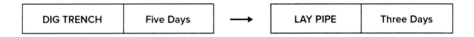

The boxes contain the name and duration of each activity, while the connecting arrow simply states that the task to the right, the successor, cannot start before the one to the left, the predecessor, has been completed. (This might in reality be an unnecessarily tight restriction. If the trench is a long one we might be able to start laying pipe before it is finished. But that's fairly advanced stuff which we'll get to later.)

But which trench? There will probably be several trenches: electric cable, water pipes, sewerage, gas, phone and TV cables. Each trench will need an identifier of some sort, and the easiest and most reliable way of doing it is to arrange for an **identifier number** (ID) to be attached to each task. Thinking ahead to the documentation (the Godot subproject), the ID shall be part of every reference to the materials to be consumed in each particular task. Thus we extend the task box to include the ID:-

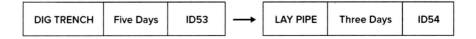

Here we have given the DIG TRENCH task an ID of 53, say, and the LAY PIPE task an ID of 54. In actual practice, the IDs will probably be just a couple of running numbers assigned during creation of the plan (about which this book will preach *ad nauseam*).

So far we have identified three fields that a task may contain. Only another 97 to go folks! We have now expanded the layout to look like this:-

Name	DU
ID	

The nucleus of the task; enough to get us started. Expanding on the idea of tasks, labelled simply by the IDs and linked by arrows, as described above, we build up a logical task network looking something like this:-

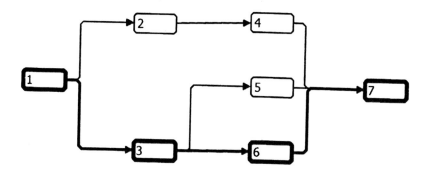

Identifying the Critical Path and Tasks by ID

Here we have identified each task by its ID only, but of course we know by now that hidden in each box there is at least a Name and a Duration (DU). Given, indeed, that each one does contain a duration, the logic will enable us to compute how long this mini project would take to carry out.

Analysing a PERT Chart

The Forward Pass

Thus our next concern is to start attaching times and dates to each task as we lay out the boxes and arrows of the plan, all in the Aristotelian logical order of the project to determine the Critical Path (see below).

In practise there are two sets of dates for an activity: the customer's and the supplier's. The earliest humanly possible and the latest we can possibly get away with. Let us suppose then that each activity contains two extra fields called **EARLIEST START** (ES) and **EARLIEST FINISH** (EF):-

Name	DU
ID	
ES	EF

To simplify the arithmetic, let us suppose that each duration is an exact number of days. Furthermore, let us say that Task ID 1 starts on the morning of day 1 and has DU of 5. It will then finish at the end of day 5. Its ES = 1 and its EF = 5.

Successor Tasks, ID 2 and 3, may start when ID 1 has finished, i.e. on the morning of day 6, each with an ES of 6.

In turn this means that if, say, Task ID 2 had a DU of 1, it would also finish on day 6, with an EF of 6, and its successor, ID 4, would have an ES of 7, starting on the morning of day 7.

Applying the same rules to the remaining tasks of the network we would eventually be able to determine the ES and EF of every task up to Task ID 7, the EF of which would be the earliest time at which the project could possibly finish.

At this point we assume, for planning purposes, that the project will actually finish on its earliest finish date, so we anchor the dates there and take the next step.

Not all earliest starts are equally early

In doing so we note that some tasks have more than one predecessor or are followed by more than one successor. This gives rise to choices of early starts, depending on the preceding earliest finishes, i.e. not all earliest starts are equally early, which allows us to choose one depending on circumstances. It is this choice which makes network planning possible, as we shall now see.

This has been the simple way of explaining the process, and you may accept it as enough to keep you going. However, if you want to follow this analysis section in detail just continue reading the chapter.

The Backward Pass

Having arrived at the last task of the network we now do something that is a little unnatural, we go backwards in time, something that has to be thought about carefully. To do this we introduce two new fields into the task panoply, **LATEST START** (LS) and **LATEST FINISH** (LF), as shown:-

Name	DU
ID	Flt
ES	EF
LS	LF

We carry out the reverse process, from right to left, at each stage working out the LF and the LS for each task, finally subtracting each early date from its corresponding late date to give us a magic number for each task called its Float (Flt), now also added to the task layout. We call this whole process the *analysis* of the network. This analysis is the basis of all project planning; all project planning computer systems are based on it, and all else is a matter of user needs and the polychromatic pictures on your computer screen.

An example of a piece of planning, showing float, as it appears on the screen, is shown in Chapter 4.

Float and the Critical Tasks

So, having computed our earliest and latest times, we can discuss the vital concept of Float, the difference between the earliest and the latest times of each task.

> **No float, no hope**

The importance of float is that it is a sort of shock absorber; up to a point, it allows preceding tasks to finish late without the delay having a domino effect with the total network, thereby delaying the final task, and the delivery of the product, leading to much gnashing of teeth, discussion of one's parentage and fiscal unhappiness. But only until the project finish date equals the LF of the final task. Beyond that you're in trouble; no float, no hope. You can say that float is a measure of the quality of a task. The greater the float of a task, the greater the chance of its success, and ultimately the greater the float of an entire project the greater the probability that it will finish successfully.

Now, be warned, the worst thing you can do to a project plan is actually use it to run a project. This is a dreadful thing to say in a book about project planning, but if reality is allowed to rear its ugly head, all the beauty and poetry of the planned dates become defenestrated.

> ## The critical paths are the manager's map through Project Wonderland

But we must eventually put the plan to work, and to do so we make use of yet two more fields, Actual Start (AS) and Actual Finish (AF).

At the start of the project there will inevitably be an array of tasks of zero float, the **critical tasks**, and as more Actual dates are entered float will be eaten up and more of the originally uncritical tasks will become critical. You'll find them coloured red on the computer screen. And every sequence of critical tasks is called a **critical path**. The critical paths are the manager's map through Project Wonderland. He doesn't have time to watch every task every day. And even in the critical world some criticality is redder than others. Indeed, the really wise manager has a Criticality Tsar stationed in the tent next door, furnished with a dedicated bike stand allowing the manager to pedal furiously off in the direction of today's reddest task.

The Full Solution

We now expand the simple network shown earlier, adding the new fields to the original ID fields. The tasks of a plan are connected by lines representing logical (time) constraints as shown in the example:-

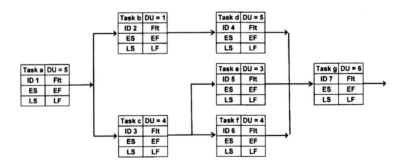

The PERT Chart

NB: in this particular PERT chart, all the constraints are of the simplest type, Finish-to-Start (FS). However, it is also possible to have Start-to-Start (SS) or Finish-to-Finish (FF) constraints, requiring several tasks to start on the same date or finish on the same date, allowing them to run in parallel.

Although carrying out an analysis is very straightforward, don't feel forced to do so yourself. You can probably see almost by instinct that it will work. However, to be certain you understand it carry out each of the steps below.

	Task	From Start of Day	DU	To End of Day
Forward Pass ==∨	a	1	5	5
	b	6	1	6
	c	6	4	9
	d	7	5	11
	e	10	3	12
	f	10	4	13
	g	14	6	19

Task	At End of Day	DU	From Start of Day	
g	19	6	14	**Backward Pass ==∨**
f	13	4	10	
e	13	3	11	
d	13	5	9	
c	9	4	6	
b	8	1	8	
a	5	5	5	

The Forward and Backward Passes

Interpreting the Solution

So far the calculated numbers are independent of particular dates and times; they are disembodied points in time. To apply them to a calendar we do the following:

Suppose Task a starts at 8 o'clock on a Monday morning, (i.e. its ES=1) then its EF of 5 means that it finishes at the end of the fifth day, a Friday, say at 5pm. But since two non-working shifts and a weekend will elapse before Task b starts, we say that for Task b: ES = 6 means it starts 8 am the following Monday, and EF = 6 means it finishes at 5pm the same day.

Similarly for Task c, EF = 9 means it finishes at 5pm on the Thursday.

And at the end of the network, Task g, EF = 19 means that it finishes at the end of working day 19, i.e. at the end of the fourth Thursday. Nineteen working days result here in 25 elapsed days. You have to be careful to distinguish between the two, making sure that your lords and masters hear you correctly when you tell them how things are going. You are going to need those weekends later on as time slips between your sweaty, frictionless fingers.

With a little bribery, you may be able to convert those elapsed days into working days. Make sure your planning system allows you to add Saturdays and Sundays to your calendars. Fortunately, most computer-based planning systems understand only too well the need for getting the troops in on a weekend.

The Critical Path

The Float (Flt) for each task, LF-EF, is as follows:

Task	LF	EF	Float
a	5	5	0
b	8	5	3
c	9	9	0
d	13	11	2
e	13	12	1
f	13	13	0
g	19	19	0

Identifying the Critical Path

The Critical Path therefore consists of Tasks a, c, f and g (Float = 0). These tasks are usually coloured red in computer planning systems, alerting the manager and the people working on them that any delay in any one of them will lead to a delay in its remaining successors, leading eventually to a delay in the entire project. Even managers have limited time, so keeping one's eye on the critical path during the implementation of a project can be a most profitable use of managerial time.

Other Resources

The only resource considered so far in this chapter is that of time. Indeed, it is the only resource each and every one of us has. We're born with it. Ironically, though, it's the one we all complain about the most. It stretches away into a usually indistinct future as an apparently infinite quantity, yet as it arrives and becomes today we suddenly complain that we don't have enough of it. It works in the opposite way to light or gravity, which increase as things get closer. But there's more to planning than time.

> **Time is the only resource each**
> **and every one of us has**

There are premises, piping, paint and people – human beings of every ilk – and the problems of getting hold of them. It is the unavailability and volatility of resources that make project management such an exciting profession, the topic of the next chapter.

Human beings of every ilk

The next chapter ...

... continues the planning process incorporating resources beyond time. Company employees. Contract labour. Skills. Scheduling. Computer systems. Screen size. Plan structure. Baseline. Politicians. Milestones. Tasks. Facilities beyond the core system.

Chapter 4: Further Elements of Project Planning: Dealing with the Visible Resources

Representation of visible things

Leonardo da Vinci

Planning Beyond Time

This chapter is also aimed at project managers and planners, but should also be of interest to anyone working the details of a project. We often get handed a work schedule that seems to lack coherence. However, there is always an explanation – though it is often difficult to disentangle.

Up to this point, the only resource we have included in the task is that of time. As we said in the previous chapter, time has the unique distinction of being the only resource that absolutely everyone has; you may be broke and living in a cardboard box, but at least you have time to do something about it – or forget about it. The next step is to introduce the topic of the more visible resources, alluded to earlier. Again, we incorporate them task by task, and all planning systems invite you to do this, providing you with large arrays of task fields in which to define them. Let us suppose they look like this:-

TASK NAME	DU	ID	ES	EF	LS	LF	RESO1	RESO2	RESO3

You may define a resource field (RESO n - where n represents a number) as anything you need to carry out this specific task: consumable resources such as steel and concrete, non-consumable such as fork-lift trucks and cranes, and premises such as offices, laboratories and test beds. But of primarily importance are the people.

Old Fred's not too busy

In the case of people, during this planning phase content yourself with codes for the types of expertise you need: engineers, electricians or elephant trainers. You may not need them until next year, and you probably won't know precisely who's going to be available. This is the strategic phase of planning. The tactics take place on or close to the day. Who's not doing anything right now? Old Fred's not too busy. Why isn't he? The eternal Mexican standoff when hiring anybody.

Human Resources

Company employees

Essentially there are two recognised sources of human resources, employees and contractors, and you need to know the pros and cons of each. The overwhelming advantage of using fellow employees on a project is that they know the company. They have probably worked on similar projects before and they know how the company works. They know all about company procedures and how best to circumvent them. They will probably know many of the other project workers, in particular the team leaders, and it all leads to a harmonious, productive atmosphere. (Or it doesn't.)

> **An essential quality of project people is their willingness to move**

But another clear advantage is that the experience gained from completed projects stays with the company.

A company's experience is the experience of its people, not of its organisation chart, its drawing registry system or the distinctive appearance of its fleet of delivery trucks. This experience resides in the minds and hands of their employees, and if their employees one day become somebody else's employees, that experience moves with them. This is trite but true, and forgotten at the company's peril. It became abundantly clear with one of the Norwegian oil platform construction companies. They had built a series of platforms in one of the fjords, but to increase production they started a second manufacturing line in a distant fjord, using different people. To the keen observer the platforms were identical; the same engineering drawings, the same materials suppliers, the same project plans, the same name on the front door, even the same logo-encrusted workers' jackets. But, the new production line cost twice the original one. The company had ignored the value of ensuring that enough human experience had been moved over to the new line; an essential quality of project people is their willingness to move.

Contract Labour

On the other hand, a significant advantage of using contract labour is that they are right there on that Monday morning; you write a contract with them, they need the work and most of the time they are in good supply. In contrast, it is like shifting sands writing internal contracts with fellow employees. "Sure, my guys will be there. Don't worry. We don't need a contract". But, on the day they are needed, they are still on their previous job. "Haven't quite finished yet. They will be with you on Thursday". Company dominoes.

Furthermore, outside contractors should have done jobs like these many times before for other customers. Therefore, they bring valuable experience with them. And you never know, at the end of the project you may be able to persuade the best of the contract workers to change jackets. Life goes on.

Temps

In addition to the recognised sources of human labour there is the untalked-about, global temporary source. I encountered them for this first time in Speyer, in Germany, while running machine trials in the Proctor and Gamble Worms project. (I should say that P&G don't sell worms, they sell soap but have a filling machine complex in the city of Worms, famous in other, historical, contexts.) Although the trials were of the machinery, some of it was (as usual) missing and we needed a bunch of fit, resourceful assistants to move stuff around the missing sections. I asked the local staff to find some people, and our team was ready waiting when the temps arrived at the appointed hour.

Cunningly, the newcomers had cleverly contrived to distinguish themselves from the company resources by the colour and quantity of their hair – as well as their psychedelic tribal attire and the artistic strands of barbed wire that adorned the visible sections of their faces. Their general appearance struck dread in the hearts of the company engineers, who backed off the scene with cries of, "You're the project manager, you deal with them!" (I wish someone could write a satisfactorily comprehensive, globally applicable job definition for the role of project manager.)

However, when in doubt one should charge the enemy (real or imaginary), with head lowered and throw them into confusion, which I did. But they allayed their gothic appearance to shake the proffered hand, wishing me luck with the job in which they had come to participate. No, they had no car parking problems. They had no car. But a spot of breakfast would add to the probability of a successful day. All in impeccable English, which is more than you can expect in many of the English projects I've come across. All they wanted was some wherewithal to support their anticipated evening's jollity.

OK gentlemen, you can come out now. (You never get a second chance to establish yourself as Banana in Chief.)

Skills

But at the planning stage you aren't going to name names. You name skills:-
RESO1 = ELECTRICAL ENGINEERS
RESO2 = MECHANICAL ENGINEERS
RESO3 = CONCRETE MIXERS
RESO4 = PLATFORM MANAGEMENT CONTROL PANEL SIMULATORS

Linked to each resource code will be the cost information: purchase price, hourly usage cost, etc. And in the case of company-employed labour it should include their availability.

The Scheduling Phase

We have identified everything we need to create the core of the plan, which is provided by all computer based planning systems; at this point they are all much of a muchness. We are now set to carry out the last set of calculations. Armed with the analysis of the network, constrained only by the logic and the single constraint of time, we now impose the constraints brought about by all these other resources to create the *schedule*.

The schedule is the complete version of the plan. It is the source of just about everything we need to know before embarking on the live project.

Scheduling comes in two flavours, resource-limited and time-limited. In resource-limited scheduling we allow as much time as it takes to carry out a set of tasks with a necessarily limited set of resources at hand, with no allowance for overtime or weekend work.

By time-limited scheduling we mean that by applying as many resources as it takes to complete a set of tasks within the analysed dates the work can be done. (The standard exceptions to this are dentistry and pregnancy.) In practice, a plan will contain a mixture of both. Where specialist resources are required they will undoubtedly be in short supply, and their activities will *ipso facto* be resource-limited. Perhaps the best example of this is that of computer programming: the world abounds in lousy computer programs written by Warm Bodies. But, we return to this in Chapter 19.

The Schedule

As we said previously, analysis of the network is concerned only with time, with no other resource involved. That is the easy part. The complications arise as soon as we start manning the tasks and cluttering them with materials, machinery, facilities, etc. People have different levels of prior experience, work at different speeds and might not be available when needed or when initially promised. Equipment breaks down and facilities burn down.

There are all sorts of reasons why physical resources are unable to match the original time required, as we all know. We therefore need to follow the analysis with a similar calculation in which we take all the other resources into consideration.

To do so we use the non-temporal resource codes (RESO...):

TASK NAME	DU	ID	ES	EF	LS	LF	RESO1	RESO2	RESO3

in which the resource code fields contain lower level fields for, for example:-

- Resource availability
- Resource requirements
- Resource prices or hire rates, etc.

The result of a scheduling process almost inevitably results in delays in task start and finish times. More precisely, we conduct a time-limited schedule, in which we hold fixed the analysed times and discover whether we have specified sufficient resources, followed by a resource-limited schedule to show us whether the analysis has allowed us sufficient time. What often happens is that there are not sufficient resources, in which case (task overload) a decision has to be taken between perhaps delaying the project finish or, if possible, applying more people to the task.

Of course, in all this we make as much use of float as possible, and it is worth remembering where a task may eat up its float without delaying the project. Another ploy to speed up a network is to fine-tune it, wherever possible, by reworking the logic to increase the amount of parallel operation

Computer-based Project Planning Systems

Until the 1970s project planning was carried out by hand on large sheets of paper stuck on the wall, with the inevitable invention of blu-tack. But times have changed. The world today is awash with computer systems to assist the project planner. Indeed, it is unthinkable these days not to use a computer and your problem will not be finding one but selecting one from the bewildering array. Each system is slightly different in appearance, but all are identical at heart; they all do exactly as described in this chapter, and will always print the same dates. However, in Chapter 5 we expand on this fundamental version of a system by supplementing it with software features, bought in from the software industry: facilities unique to your organisation.

To complete this chapter, then, let us run our PERT chart through a typical system to turn the day numbers into dates. The plan tasks have the following layout:-

TASK NAME	DURATION
ID	FLOAT
EARLY START	EARLY FINISH
LATE START	LATE FINISH

Let us start Task a on the first working Monday of 2010, 4th January, giving us the following picture:-

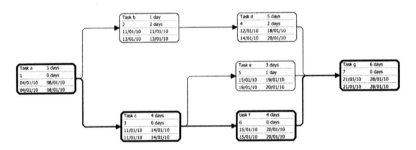

Identifying the Critical tasks with Zero Float

This printout has a format typical of most standard planning systems available on the market. The critical tasks, each with a Float of zero, are shown with thick borders. The thin-bordered boxes are the non-critical tasks. The total working time is computed simply by adding the durations along the critical path, 19 days. The analysis shows the mini-plan as finishing on 28th January, having taken the weekends into consideration; a total duration of 25 elapsed days. All straightforward stuff.

Your Tiny Window on the Project World

However, there are three problems with the PERT picture presentation of the plan. One is that the restricted size of the ordinary screen limits the number of tasks that can be displayed, say about a dozen at a time. A partial solution to this problem is to splash out on a second screen in tandem with your primary screen. In this way, you can double the number of viewable tasks. Another is to have a magic button reduce the box size to that of the ID version illustrated in Chapter 3. This would provide for some hundred displayed tasks on a single screen, allowing us to follow the logic; any single box clickable to reveal the hidden detail, eg ID7:-

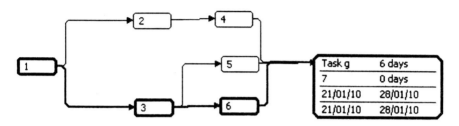

A Critical Path in Simplified Format

The second problem is that although you may have a hundred column fields available for display on the screen, there is a severe limit to the number available at any one time. This discussion is taken up in Chapter 11.

The third problem is that box size doesn't represent task duration, DU; though logic is easy to see, magnitude isn't. To solve this we can represent each task by a bar rather than a box, moving the fields to a separate area of the screen. We call this a logic bar chart:-

Task Name	Duration	Planned Start	Planned Finish	Float	04 Jan '10	11 Jan '10	18 Jan '10	25 Jan '10
					S M T W T F S	S M T W T F S	S M T W T F S	S M T W T
Task a	5 days	04/01/10	08/01/10	0 days				
Task b	1 day	11/01/10	11/01/10	2 days				
Task c	4 days	11/01/10	14/01/10	0 days				
Task d	5 days	12/01/10	18/01/10	2 days				
Task e	3 days	15/01/10	19/01/10	1 day				
Task f	4 days	15/01/10	20/01/10	0 days				
Task g	6 days	21/01/10	28/01/10	0 days				

A Logic Bar Chart

In this picture, the bars depict the calendar duration and the arrows the logic. The critical task bars are white, and each non-critical (hashed) bar is shown starting at its earliest start date. Clearly each can start later without going critical provided it finishes by the latest finish date, LF. In the calculations a weekend is not part of the Float, so your weekends allow you to catch up, and this is particularly important if the project takes place far from home where there's nothing to do at weekends. So, to increase your probability of a successful project, hold it miles away from home.

**To increase your probability of a successful
project, hold it miles away from home**

NB, in a bar chart view a tandem screen would allow you to triple the number of viewable fields, since the bars occupy only about half of one screen.

There can be much more information associated with each task, though only some six are displayed in the above diagram.[3] Different arrangements of fields may be displayed, as required, by clicking a button.

Plan Structure

As we said at the start of this chapter, it is aimed at senior, non-detail people, who are unlikely to get involved in the planning process to a significant degree. However, they are nevertheless interested in specific information when problems occur; they might be the owner of a project, or

---

[3] To the left of the bar field.

a major part thereof, or the customer for whom the project is being carried out. To make it easy for the detail man to explain things to the generalist, computer planning systems provide for hierarchical planning as shown in the following Strategy plan.

Suppose you have a top, strategic level consisting of a few all-encompassing tasks, each covering a substantial period of time, a major component of the product or an engineering speciality, say. Suppose we name them Strategic 1, Strategic 2 etc. On sheet one of the Planning Document they could appear thus:-

ID	Task Name	Duration	Planned Start	Planned Finish	Jan '10	Feb '10	Mar '10	Apr '10	May
					28 04 11 18 25	01 08 15 22	01 08 15 22	29 05 12 19 26	03
1	Strategic 1	55 days	04/01/10	19/03/10					
2	Strategic 2	33 days	22/03/10	05/05/10					
3	Strategic 3	21 days	18/01/10	15/02/10					
4	Strategic 4	30 days	25/01/10	05/03/10					
5	Strategic 5	18 days	01/02/10	24/02/10					

Sheet One of the Planning Document

This diagram doesn't tell you very much. The detail is all hidden inside the black bars; almost none of the logic is showing. But, it does show the manager where his part of the action sits; it shows him where to start. He asks the project manager what's going wrong with his part of the action, Strategic 1 say. His guess might be that it lies in the early part of the plan, so the project manager hits the Drill Down button to show that it consists of three components of the next level, Level 1:-

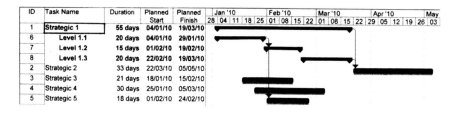

ID	Task Name	Duration	Planned Start	Planned Finish	Jan '10	Feb '10	Mar '10	Apr '10	May
					28 04 11 18 25	01 08 15 22	01 08 15 22	29 05 12 19 26	03
1	Strategic 1	55 days	04/01/10	19/03/10					
6	Level 1.1	20 days	04/01/10	29/01/10					
7	Level 1.2	15 days	01/02/10	19/02/10					
8	Level 1.3	20 days	22/02/10	19/03/10					
2	Strategic 2	33 days	22/03/10	05/05/10					
3	Strategic 3	21 days	18/01/10	15/02/10					
4	Strategic 4	30 days	25/01/10	05/03/10					
5	Strategic 5	18 days	01/02/10	24/02/10					

One Level Down in the Planning Document

Still not enough detail? OK, hit the Drill Down button once again to get the next level, Level 1.1:-

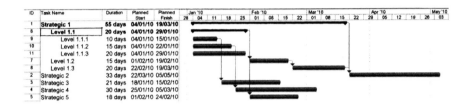

Two Levels Down in the Planning Document

We're now down to the working level. This third picture is probably enough to illustrate the point.

> **Letting there be light can take more than the canonical six days**

In a well-structured plan, this process can continue down to a level at which the planner has felt it worthwhile doing. It takes time to plan, and although managers want the detail to show when the chips are down, they are most reluctant to allow time to plan at the outset. "Get on with it!" "Get on with what?!" The eternal conflict between master and slave. It's OK for some saying, let there be light. Letting there be light can take more than the canonical six days.

The Baseline

The project plan will, in practise, take more iterations to complete than you would like and the final version will almost certainly contain items of contention. Technical people love to fine-tune and perhaps the most prolific fine-tuner was Walt Disney. At the start of it all he was the artist and he was forever reworking Mickey Mouse's ears and nose. Fortunately, for him he had somehow surrounded himself with people with a stake in the nascent company but happily with no ability to draw. To them, Mickey's ears and noses were of lesser importance than the pranks he got up to. "C'mon Walt, let's get this stuff on the road; there's a generation of deprived kids out there, all waiting for a termination of their deprivation". "Hold it you guys, you don't have this vision. You can't see the ultimate mouse. He's got to be friendlier. Give my pencil just another twenty-four hours". Finally the boys got their way, but if you look carefully at the very earliest comics you will see that he was right. They evolved month by month into the ultimate mouse. On the other hand, had he had his way he would have been a poverty-stricken perfectionist doing caricatures with not even a footnote in our cultural history.

Eventually you have to agree that there are degrees of perfection, and unless you are in the space business you are going to have to do a little compromising. Even in space you wouldn't today use the simple computers that were used to get us onto the moon and back in the sixties – but they did the job, and could do so again if they had to. I often wonder how the astronauts would have felt had they known then that they were being transported by less computer power than would be contained in a next-generation kids' gaming computer.

So here's your opportunity of influencing things. Somehow, you have to call a halt to the planning and get out your "holy water". But that's what managers are paid to do. And how you do it is entirely up to you: I don't get your salary.

However, what I can do for you is the sprinkling. This consists of creating the Baseline. The plan Baseline is the final version obtained at five o'clock in the evening of the day your patience finally runs out. The next working day is day zero, the first day of the live project, and the baseline is the version against which all live versions from that day are compared. It looks like this:-

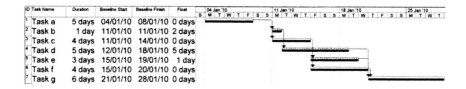

ID	Task Name	Duration	Baseline Start	Baseline Finish	Float
1	Task a	5 days	04/01/10	08/01/10	0 days
2	Task b	1 day	11/01/10	11/01/10	2 days
3	Task c	4 days	11/01/10	14/01/10	0 days
4	Task d	5 days	12/01/10	18/01/10	5 days
5	Task e	3 days	15/01/10	19/01/10	1 day
6	Task f	4 days	15/01/10	20/01/10	0 days
7	Task g	6 days	21/01/10	28/01/10	0 days

Baseline versus Live Version

Here you see two new date columns, Baseline Start and Baseline Finish, while each task bar now consists of two split bars, the upper one, white or shaded (critical or not), constitutes the living, breathing plan, updated day by day as progress is made, and the lower, grey, one is the immutable baseline version of each task plan. Let us suppose, now, that Task c has a delayed start on the 14th instead of the planned 11th:-

ID	Task Name	Duration	Actual Start	Baseline Start	Baseline Finish	Float
1	Task a	5 days	NA	04/01/10	08/01/10	3 days
2	Task b	1 day	NA	11/01/10	11/01/10	2 days
3	Task c	4 days	14/01/10	11/01/10	14/01/10	0 days
4	Task d	5 days	NA	12/01/10	18/01/10	5 days
5	Task e	3 days	NA	15/01/10	19/01/10	1 day
6	Task f	4 days	NA	15/01/10	20/01/10	0 days
7	Task g	6 days	NA	21/01/10	28/01/10	0 days

Impact of Delaying a Task

Because Task c was critical at the start, we see that the tasks of the critical path have been pushed forward, causing the entire project to be moved out, delayed by three working days.

Depicting the baseline in this way shows the project manager, and the massed spectators peering over his shoulder, to what extent the project has been delayed. We return to the discussion of the baseline in Chapter 6.

A Note to Politicians

As a case in point, one of the worst computer projects of all time, still far from complete, clocking up cost but doing little, is the British National Health Service "Spine" project (described in Chapter 20). As I write, it is costing over £12billion, but it is impossible to discuss its progress with any degree of objectivity simply because the perpetrators did not save a Baseline. The Commons Select Committee has no objective way of knowing whether or not the implementation is fulfilling requirements. Indeed, they may not even know what the requirements are. They are playing football without the aid of goalposts. The one thing that any politician sitting on a project review committee must say is, show me the Baseline.[4] Sadly they rarely do.

Milestones

A project of substantial size can often be thought of as a collection of subprojects, bound together both contractually and logically. The way a full project can be sliced depends very much on the nature of the deliverables and the extent to which the subprojects can be run smoothly in parallel, in order to minimise completion time. As an example, an aircraft consists of such major components as body, wings, tail plane and engines. Each of these can be (and is) built separately, often by different suppliers in different parts of the world. The key here is to have each of these components delivered at the right time at the final assembly plant. That right time we call a milestone, and each mini project will have a manager whose main responsibility will be to watch that milestone like a hawk. But, how do we organise the plan to promulgate the milestones?

Starting at the top, an easy way to show this is to make use of the earlier Strategy network, replacing the top-level bars with Milestones:-

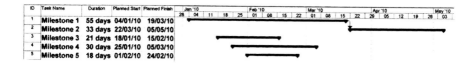

Milestones in a Strategy Network

Now, to keep this illustration simple, supposing each milestone is the responsibility of a single company department, with perhaps each department manager as its owner, they might be assigned as follows:-

---

4   *Post Script: On 23rd July, 2011, as part of my correspondence with the Depart-ment of Health, I received a letter stating that my correspondent wasn't sure what a Baseline was. This is not a guarantee that no one else connected with the project knew what it was, but it might explain a great deal.*

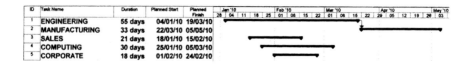

Milestones For Key Departments

Thus, each milestone owner would be able to check the progress of his range of the plan. In turn, as an example, the Engineering Department may consist of further subdivisions:-

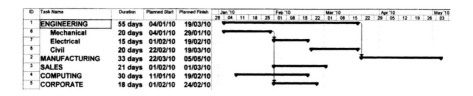

Milestones Within Key Departments

And down to the working level, Mechanical Engineering might consist of drawings, weights and ordering:-

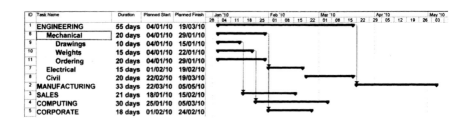

Milestones Within Key Departments, Drilled Down

In reality, at the outset there are no dates. These are the result, of course, of the detailed planning, section by section. During the running of the project, which we take up in Chapter 11, this technique allows us to "drill down" to the level of interest.

Other Types of Constraint

So far, in our explanations of constraints we have restricted ourselves to Finish-to-Start (FS) constraints, without saying much about them. This type of constraint says that the preceding task must complete before the successor is capable of starting. But this isn't always true. There can be Start-to-Start (SS) and Finish-to-Finish (FF) constraints, and even Start-to-Finish (SF), though the latter can be a bit contrived. An SS constraint means that neither task can start until both can start. The reason for requiring this arrangement would be that both tasks are interrelated in some way.

A more interesting and frequently used one is the FF constraint: both tasks finishing at the same time – with perhaps a short planned delay between them. Suppose you are building a fence using a carpenter and a painter. The painter doesn't have to wait until the carpentry is finished before starting to paint. He can start as soon as there's enough distance between both workmen so that the carpenter doesn't get paint on his overalls. So, say that the carpentry takes ten days and the painting six, this is what this bit of planning would look like:-

ID	Task Name	Duration	Planned Start	Planned Finish
1	Deliver materials	3 days	25/07/11	27/07/11
2	Carpentry	10 days	28/07/11	10/08/11
3	Painting	6 days	03/08/11	10/08/11

Planning for the Carpentry and Painting

Here we have the carpentry task following the delivery of the materials, with the painting starting as soon as possible but both fence tasks finishing together. However, since this gives us the problem of the painter catching up with the carpenter on the last day we can add a one-day, say, delay in the painting:-

ID	Task Name	Duration	Planned Start	Planned Finish	25 Jul '11							01 Aug '11							08 Aug '11					
					S	M	T	W	T	F	S	S	M	T	W	T	F	S	S	M	T	W	T	F
1	Deliver materials	3 days	25/07/11	27/07/11																				
2	Carpentry	10 days	28/07/11	10/08/11																				
3	Painting	6 days	04/08/11	11/08/11																				

Making Adjustments to the Carpentry and Painting

Managing the Task

You now have a fair idea of what a task is. As part of the body of a plan, it bears a distinct similarity to a cell in an animal body, like a cell it is a plan in its own right; a mini plan. It will comprise at least one person, though very often more, and an assembly of non-human resources, all requiring time and money and all constituting a potential threat to the plan as a whole. So if it is large or complex enough it may need a mini project manager, a Task Manager, responsible for ensuring the task is carried out. This could be the project manager himself, acting down, or one of the people actually working on the task. Or it could be someone perhaps responsible for a particular set of tasks, all perhaps working together in a particular phase of the plan. Or it could be someone responsible for a component of the WBS; each such component is the physical output of a group of tasks. Thus, it would be more complete to append a code for the Task Manager, TM, right there in the task:-

TASK NAME	DU	ID	ES	EF	LS	LF	RESOs	TM

We return to the discussion of the Task Manager in Chapter 6.

Beyond the Core

This chapter has described the core elements of most project planning systems. However, as we said earlier in the chapter, you may expand your core system with functions peculiar to your unique organisation.

The next chapter ...

...discusses components of the planning system outside the universal core. Corporate intrusion. Human Resources. Suppliers Register. Drawing Register. Verbal Documents. Timesheets. Plan amplification companies.

Chapter 5: Coping With Planning Details Outside the Core

Corroborative detail, intended to give artistic verisimilitude

Gilbert and Sullivan

All Companies are Different

This chapter does not abound with arithmetic. Rather it deals with managerial issues such as the design of the corporate computing system. Hopefully, high amongst potential readers will be people in the computing systems design department.

So far, we have described the nature of a typical planning system, the nucleus of your individual corporate system. Thus, this chapter is about project activity not handled immediately by your project planning software. It is therefore of paramount interest to the project manager, whose initial task is to create the plan. Every project is different in detail. Every company operates differently. Every manager manages differently – and, by the very nature of projects, project managers have the broadest terms of reference in which to operate. Since no software system can possibly cover everything there will always be something you'd like to have that isn't there. This gap between the core of planning as described in the previous chapters and the full panoply is slowly closing, but there is still much to be done. This gap has not gone unnoticed by some very talented software companies, most of them comprising very small but highly competent groups of programmers.

The Corporate Intrusion

But firstly, a word about traditional corporate computer systems and the intrusion of project planning systems. Project management software has traditionally been brought in as something of an afterthought in most companies, and often by people who are remote from the central computing department.

There is very little project management culture in most project-operating companies

The corporate headquarters might be in Houston while the project might be in Saudi Arabia. Typical company program suites consist of customer lists, employee details, payroll, accounts payable and receivable, general accounting, parts and materials receivable, goods outwards and deliverables and so on. All well known company functions.

The reason why project management has always been a sort of Cinderella is that there is, unbelievably, very little project management culture in most project-operating companies. Projects don't appear on the organisation charts – if for no other reason than they don't last long enough to gain attention. Organisation charts are the result of much expensive pontification upon high and sadly project managers rarely get the management spotlight needed to appear in the promotion queue. But perhaps the main reason for lack of integration of the project software into the traditional software is that it doesn't enjoy the rhythmic company attention required of the payroll system and its associated phenomena. Anyway, project folk are different, and traditional employees don't understand them. Indeed, the Neolithic traditionalists run away from the Palaeolithic experimentalists should the latter ever have the temerity to show up.

**Neolithic traditionalists running away
from Palaeolithic experimentalists**

So such systems as the Drawing Register, the Suppliers Register, Timekeeping, Goods Received and Payroll are not part of most project management software. But you'd like them to be: gaps in the corporate information panoply are sources of much error and consternation. You need a holistic computer, not an assembly of computer gimmicks. You'd like planning to be a fluent activity, uninterrupted by phone grabbing, bicycle leaping or searching through ancient planning documents in vain efforts to find names and addresses of resources used in the past; all should have finger-tip accessibility.

Obtaining the Human Resources

In Chapter 4 we discussed the pros and cons of using employees versus contractors to man the tasks. We know how to get hold of employees from our associated departments, don't we?! But, how can we use the computer to help us find contractors? The first occasion on which any lacking feature will show itself is when you start to man the tasks with workers. The plan has been satisfactorily analysed and you will now want to start thinking about who is going to do it all – the human resources. Whether they are going to be fellow employees or mercenaries from a consulting company, you would like to know right now whether there will be enough telephone sanitizers available on or close to the analysed dates. You are sitting at your screen, planning, and you want to stay there. In the old days, and still today to some extent, you had to get on your bike and go out begging and haggling with the euphemistic suppliers. But that's not the way we'd like to do things. You want immediate access to the Suppliers Register (the SR), an online, real-time availability database.

You type in Telephone Sanitizers and the register comes up with a spread of such specialists available at about the planned dates, with coded qualifications, prices, etc. Not necessarily by name but certainly in terms of offers of availability from their employing departments or companies. At this stage, you may be only able to play a numbers game to demonstrate the viability of the project, or you may have reached the serious stage of manning up a live project, in which case you will want to be able to email a contract to the supplying company or department. In principle, you should be able to man up the task in minutes, an exchange of e-mails accepted as a contract. But what does such a feature look like?

The Suppliers Register (SR)

On your screen, you have a (soft) SR button. You have selected the relevant task, displaying the fields required for the current item of interest. Everything the suppliers will need to know is contained in the task fields. All you need do is click on the SR button and e-mails are dispatched forthwith to all suppliers of telephone sanitizers. You'd like to be buried in availability, and you could well be. So behind the scenes in the availability software you will have worked out a priority schedule with the software suppliers; either that or you scan the incoming lists by eye and select them on the screen for acceptance. That's up to you. You know your suppliers. Also hidden from view will be a contract to come into play when the due day arrives, bearing in mind that things get delayed even in the best of plans. Both sides know this and you will want to minimise the propensity to haggle.

The Drawing Register (DR)

Another function that you'd like to have automated is the Drawing Register, enabled by the DR button. Every design drawing is created in connection with the activity specified within one or other task in the plan. Of course, not every task produces a drawing; some tasks may produce more than one drawing, and some drawings could be the result of the work of more than one task; the task-drawing relationship can be one-to-one or one-to-many.

> **Has someone forgotten to plan the entire landing gear?**

That doesn't matter. What matters is that every drawing shall bear at least one task number, which the drawing sheet shall contain and which the draughtsman uses to inform the task that work has started and eventually that work has finished. If the draughtsman cannot locate a task number from the plan it has to mean that something is missing. So, what else has gone wrong? What else is missing? Is this just a momentary lapse or has someone forgotten to plan the entire landing gear? So not only does the online drawing register enable fluent reporting into the plan, it is a valuable catalyst for ensuring completeness of the plan – a function not of negligible value.

The Written Documents

And what is good for the drawings is equally good for the verbal documents. Let every document bear a task number; every letter (e or snail), every contractual item, every delivery note, and every paragraph in the managerial reports. So you need a DOC button. As each task-generated document is issued, the task number magically appears at the top left hand corner of the screen and the printed page, and its reference gets copied into the associated DOC database. These are the details of using the plan as the Spine document, as described in Chapter 14.

Easy access to documentation is fundamentally important

The Timesheet Function

But how about the Timesheet function? Since your payroll system needs precisely the same basic information for computing the salaries as the project system needs for assessing the man-hours expended on each task, it makes a lot of sense to arrange for the salary data to be copied into the project plan. The basic data feeds into two detailed applications, of course. The one is attached to salary rates, etc and is sent eventually to the bank, while the other is fanned out into the tasks on which the work has been done, and instead of computed into actual financial amounts is probably converted to standard costs for telephone sanitizers etc. This data has several uses, for example to compare actual amounts with planned estimates and to provide an on-going prediction of task completion date. The latter can also be used to compute percent complete, the purpose of which is to give management both an emotional feel for how things are going and to provide the basis for part payments for work done on incomplete tasks. NB: If non-payable time is allowed to be registered to the project, the program needs to be told this: this is part of the program specification. We take this up in detail in Chapter 6.

Plan Amplification Companies

There are several companies who provide such amplifications of the standard planning systems. You can find their details on the Internet, but two particularly successful examples are the resource management company, Innate Management Systems Ltd, and the contact tracking company, Project Support Ltd – or you could ask me.

The next chapter ...

... discusses completing the plan. Signatures. Cash flow. Baseline. Earned value. Variation Orders. Percent Complete. Plan-WBS integration. Milestones (again). Statistical management.

Chapter 6: Completing the Plan

For it is commonly said, completed labours are pleasant

Cicero

The Final Version

Here is the final round of completing the plan, with major emphasis on the relationship between company managements, in particular, finance departments. This should be of primary interest to the senior management as well as the project owner and manager.

At this stage the plan has incorporated all the customer contractual requirements and to all intents and purposes it looks complete. But it still lacks one vital component, an agreement on when to pay. The total price has been agreed, perhaps based on the prices of the constituent components of the WBS. But when should the customer actually make payments?

Getting the Task Manager's Signature

You will inevitably iterate the plan, possibly many times, before obtaining an initial live version that everybody concerned within the company will agree to. The plan will be the best compromise you can make between managerial capacity, availability of resources, customer requirements, profitability and what you allow yourself from experience of disasters past. We now need to discuss the contractual consequences of the plan that must be agreed to before it can be considered complete.

This is where I think the Managing Director should come back into the game. The computer man needs to know how to actuate the management decisions, but the computer system must allow for senior management to be in charge.

Each task has a task manager, the TM, as described in Chapter 4, someone responsible for getting the work done, and each task manager will probably be responsible for a number of tasks: perhaps a complete component of the WBS.

> ## All the signatures in the world are
> ## no guarantee of success

Obtaining the signatures of the task managers is the best hope you have of success. However, all the signatures in the world are no guarantee of success but without them you have no comeback when the going gets tough.

Essentially, you should have obtained commitment at the initial planning meetings, but *Homo sapiens* is renowned for bouts of amnesia, and you really need confirmation that when their several contributions were combined into a single entity it still made sense and was still realisable.

To make this easy, your computer system should be able to group the tasks by TM code. If then each task manager receives the complete plan not only can he see clearly what is expected of him, but also what he can expect of the others. And the fact that the several components come from a single source prevents contradictions; each knows that the others are meshed in logically.

... an undertaking that Charlie won't be on vacation

A signature means that the project and task managers understand what is to be done, that they, in turn, have an undertaking that Charlie won't be on vacation or otherwise engaged when the time comes, that they in turn have the guarantees of the people to do the work, as well as equipment, material and premises. It's a very tall order, and in practice very few project managers have the luxury of guarantees of anything before embarking on their projects. But computer technology at least makes it easier to see what is needed, what it is they aren't signing, if they aren't.

The Cash Flow Problem

The last thing we need to do in completing the plan then is to agree on how you are going to get your money as soon as possible: the problem of interim payments for work performed by the supplier prior to the termination of the project. If the project is to take place over a considerable period you could well experience cash-flow problems; you need enough cash to tide yourself over until the client releases the full contractual amount.

The problem with costs is that everyone wants to be paid – right now. We have to pay our staff and the mercenaries. Deliveries of parts and materials are accompanied by bills. We have to pay rent for work places, and so on. All well-known stuff. It is a trivial matter to aggregate the cost of carrying out the project because everything is computerised – and is probably fairly accurate; but the money flows out of the window and there's nothing we can do about it. And as it does so, a considerable amount of expense might have been incurred on a task before it is complete, with a corresponding mountain of costs building up in the accounts department. You'd like to shove that mountain out of the door as soon as possible; you'd like to convert your outlays into hard cash – but who's going to pay for half a bridge? You'd like to get hold of some of that money before you have finished the job. Is it possible to build this into the plan?

But who's going to pay for half a bridge?

Earned Value

As work is done, and money expended, the value of the work will hopefully increase, so the plan must provide the basis for the contractor to bill the client. And this must be incorporated into the plan. It must contain some sort of formula for calculating the earned value, in contrast to the accumulated cost. There must be no cause for debate after the starter's gun. So how is this done?

The final iteration of the plan, then, is the Payment Round, a planning meeting between the top levels of both customer and supplier at which a series (say, six-monthly) of Pay Points is agreed to, combined with a procedure for reviewing progress and performing the billing calculations, based on earned value. The goal shall be as little surprise as possible at the Pay Points. In principle, a Pay Point is a top brass meeting, but if you do battle successfully at the Payment Round the Pay Points could be run by lower level employees. The Pay Points also become a useful control mechanism over project management.

The fundamental Mexican standoff with earned value is that the best ploy for the supplier is to get the entire project paid for at the signing of the contract, while that of the customer is to pay for all of it on the day it's delivered and has satisfied the acceptance tests. In real life, however, neither stand is tenable; partial payments have to be made, enabling both parties to carry on in business.

Variation Orders

The goal of the supplier is to make the value of the work exceed the cost of doing it. However, if you fail to achieve this from time to time you will do what you can to obtain an adjustment to the contract. All such changes should be reported as soon as possible to the system, and made the subject of Variation Orders (VOs), a euphemism for holding out your cap. However, often the fault lies with the customer, who might have changed his design and requires a rework. And often the management of VOs becomes a major factor in a project management system. It shouldn't, but it does.

The simplest basis, of course, for the supplier billing the client is for completed work only, item by item in the WBS. Earned values would then be zero until completion and would then jump to the agreed price for that item. But far too often, especially in long-term projects, it is found to be impossible to complete one item before other items are at or near completion, with the consequence that the contractor suffers an undue delay in payment. To allow the contractor to survive until final completion and handover we need something a little softer; but something based on very rigorous planning to prevent interminable fights.

Revisions to the plan

And now we come to the humiliating admission that the immutability of a project plan is in fact OK only up to a point.

> ## The plan shall be born again

The plan of a large project, one lasting over, say, two years, will inevitably experience a progressive deterioration from the Baseline, and the time arrives when the accumulation of minor disasters becomes major enough to render the signed Baseline useless for continued management purposes. The plan shall be born again; revision one of the Baseline; perhaps the first of a series of six-monthly revisions. We have to admit that revisions are perfectly respectable, and are indeed standard practice, but each should be the result of some high-level pontification: they must not just happen. They provide management of both customer and supplier with an opportunity of appraising the situation, in particular of reviewing the contract.

The problem in the bad old days was that management at the rarefied levels found it very difficult to determine why things were the way they were, and such meetings were often therefore not uncharged with emotion. But a good computer system can help change all that, substituting information for opinion.

Adding the Incommensurable

And here we come to the Chinese mirrors bit. At the task level, management has an excellent understanding of what is going on. Each task has a well-defined start. Its progress will be paved with reports and pictures, all systematically numbered, and possibly tangible measurable objects. The costs will be accurately collected, and when the task is finished the computer will be told so. Getting it all right is the tangible stuff of project management. But as you combine tasks into larger and larger units in the WBS it becomes progressively more difficult to measure and therefore to understand. If some tasks are finished ahead of time, some on time and some behind time are you in total ahead of the game or not? What does it mean to add, in some way, the progress being made on disparate parts of the whole? If the cost to date is below schedule is it because of your brilliant fiscal control, or is it because you can get neither the stuff nor the staff?

> **You can't just add wiring and plumbing or wood and concrete**

Clearly, you need a strategic picture of the cost tied in with a strategic picture of what you have done with the money. Hence a way of depicting macroscopic progress in the light of a picture of the Baseline. But what does a macroscopic picture of the Baseline look like? The problem is that of having to add the incommensurable. You can't just add wiring and plumbing or wood and concrete. You can only add numbers derived from these actions and materials.

But what numbers? Their weights? Their cost per kilo? The number of days to go to completion? The number of man-days of effort? The prices of undelivered parts? And so on. Somehow it all has to be reduced to a common denominator, and this is bound to be fairly arbitrary and subject to judgement. The trick is to exercise the judgement at as low a level as possible, and clothe the judgement in a formula; make it look at the higher levels as though it isn't judgement. Above all, don't give the lawyers any scope for exercising their judgement. At the end of the day, it must become part of the contract and part of the project plan.

Percent Complete

The traditional yardstick, for want of something better, is the notion of percent complete. (If you find something better, let me know.) Once this is defined, you have the basis for earned value. The basic idea is illustrated by the following example. If you estimated ten man-days to do a job, and you have used five, provided your estimate was correct the job is 50% complete. By somehow aggregating the percent complete of the disparate tasks, you could calculate the percent complete of the whole. But immediately you are overwhelmed by a welter of objections. Suppose you original estimates were wrong. You might well not know this at the apparent 50% point. However, by the original 80% point you might have found that you were really only 40% complete, and the original estimate had to be doubled.

To press home the problem of percent complete, is your house 100% complete? What is it then? And what does your spouse say?

Is your house build 100% complete?

Even supposing you can measure accurately the progress of an individual task, how can you combine several? How can you add 50% of one task to 40% of another? Is the result 45%? Or should you somehow weight them in proportion to their individual cost? Fifty percent of a $10,000 task plus 40% of a $20,000 might come to a combined 43% complete. But what does it mean physically? Does it tell you anything? Could it be the basis for creating an invoice?

Anyway, how do you measure? Is money spent or man-hours consumed indicative? Is value proportional to cost? How about drawings? If you are expecting twenty drawings does ten mean 50%? Only if they are similar in size and difficulty. How about components in a WBS structure? How do you add bolts and batteries? Cranks and camshafts? What is the purpose of the upper levels of the WBS? Why do we perform these numerical gymnastics? Can we not restrict reviews to the PERT level, where progress is more meaningful?

The question is of course rhetorical. It would mean the upper levels of management abdicating all responsibility. But remember, percent complete means what you define it to mean; what for contractual purposes you and your client define it to mean. So cut the cackle and try using the method described below as the basis for periodic billing. Read it slowly, and read it twice. Then try to explain it to your boss. I have tried to make a simple explanation of an inevitably complicated problem.

The Baseline

When all the above has been satisfactorily incorporated into the plan the initial version shall be frozen in the computer. We defined this in Chapter 4 as the Baseline, the immutable (ha, ha) target with which all subsequent progress is compared. The Actuals v. Baseline report is the bottom line report as the project progresses. This report is the one report that absolutely everyone concerned with the project should read. Sadly, interest in this report is inversely proportional to altitude within a company.

Marrying the Plan to the Work Breakdown Structure (WBS)

And now we can combine the PERT chart with the WBS it is intended to implement. Of course, work needs to be done at all levels of the WBS, but most of it is done at the bottom level: components get larger and fewer until the last bolt is forced into the last hole. So let us demonstrate how this integration is done at the bottom level; the figure is an attempt at depicting the fundamental relationship between the two. As we said earlier, we may think of the WBS as the vertical object, and the PERT chart as the horizontal, as shown in the diagram:-

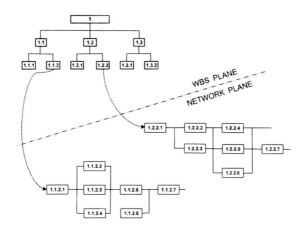

Marrying the WBS coding to the PERT chart

Here we have carried over the WBS coding to the network coding by adding a further digit, so that any particular task or group of tasks can be automatically identified with its WBS element. (Of course, any task at this level can be represented as a set of subtasks if appropriate.)

This is perhaps a rather simplistic picture. In actual practice, especially in large and complicated structures, it may not be easy to establish a strict one-to-one correspondence, but it is a goal well worth trying for as the plan is built up.

At the freezing of the network, the Baseline is aggregated up the WBS as labour and non-labour cost per component. At this stage all times are pure estimates.

Experience beats theory every time

However, during the life of the project, as experience is gained with the work, management could get the impression that the initial task durations were rather optimistic. Experience beats theory every time, and it may become clear that a new estimate of the *Remaining Duration* (RDU) of a task might exceed the current one. Better to admit the earlier optimism and redefine the Remaining Duration for percent completion purposes. Thus let the new percent complete of an individual task be defined as the number of man-hours expended to date divided by the **latest estimate** of the total man-hours required: i.e. if the latter is increased, the percent complete will actually decrease, giving the impression of negative work. In this way, however, percent complete can never exceed 100.

One cunning ploy here is for the system to automatically reach for contingency funds every time there is an increase in the Remaining Duration.

The figure shows the initial estimates of a WBS at the start of the work, and how the aggregation is performed on the costs. The percent complete of each WBS component at the bottom level can then be the total number of man-hours expended to date on the tasks leading to that component, divided by the total current estimates for those tasks. However, the percent complete values at the higher levels is a matter for agreement during the Payment Round negotiations. And for billing purposes the earned value can be defined as a predetermined fraction of the percent complete multiplied by the agreed completed value of the component.

Each triple of numbers is as follows:-

Est. LAB COST	Est. MAT COST	PERCENT COMP

Thus a WBS aggregation would look like this:-

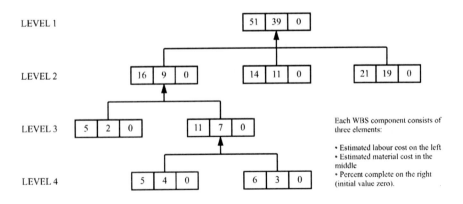

A Work Breakdown schedule Aggregation

Each WBS component consists of three elements, estimated labour cost on the left, estimated material cost in the middle and percent complete on the right (initial value zero).

The same definition can be extended, level by level, to the top, remembering that at any Pay Point the percent complete can actually decrease, despite an increase in the work done; you are always working with the latest estimates of the durations and effort. After all, these are much more accurate than those of the original plan. One thing you certainly gain as you make progress is an understanding of what it's all about. You may not be finished yet, but for certain you will have learnt a lot. Plough that sobering experience back into the management numbers as you acquire it, and be honest about it.

The top level components of the WBS become the management milestones of the project: major chunks of official progress that are fully paid for upon completion, but that can be partially paid for before completion – provided for in the contract. But these will also be part of Baseline revisions as overruns are absorbed.

Statistical Management

As a footnote to the discussion of the Project Baseline, my personal feeling is that senior managers confine themselves far too readily to high-level statistical management. Statistics often blur the vision. The broad view all too easily blinds you to individual elements that can sabotage the whole caboodle. A potential saboteur can be a very insignificant item in the total picture if you judge it solely on cost; for the want of a nail an empire was lost. The nails are deep down in the network, so when the mumbo-jumbo about percents complete is over, management should be asking questions down at the PERT level. Here's where you find the undiluted information. And if it's critical it's coloured red. The ultimate question is, which single task is furthest behind? The computer will tell you, and you can then jump on your bike and be a real manager for once.

You can be a true manager for once

The next chapter ...

... Consists of a list of a hundred factors the candidate for project manager should be confident of before accepting the job. Remove one at your peril. If you add one, let me know. And the PI, the most important of the project documents.

Chapter 7: The Project Initiation Checklist

I've got a little list

Gilbert and Sullivan

On the Art of Successful Management

Before anyone dare accept the responsibility of managing a project they must know in substantial detail what they are letting themselves in for. Thus, this chapter is of primary concern for the potential project manager, and it is up to the project owner to mastermind the process described herein. This project initiation checklist identifies all the issues that need to be tackled.

In Chapter 2, I described the very complicated sequence of events comprising the initiation of a project. In the event of your being invited to become manager of a project; the essence of project initiation is set out as a list of questions aimed to protect you. Ignore any one of them at your peril. No answers are provided because they are all different, one project to the next. But by searching for the answers you should be able to stumble on the right questions. The art of successful project management is asking them. When you are reasonably sure that you have covered each question adequately and that the answers are sufficiently encouraging, then go ahead and accept the brief. But please, not until then.

Definition and Preamble

According to the Project Management Institute the purpose of Project Initiation is to authorise the planning phase of the project. More specifically, it is the tangible output of the initiation process, the Project Charter perhaps, and establishes the Objectives, Scope and Constraints of the project.

Project Initiation covers the time from a potential manager being asked to head up a project until the living, breathing project finally starts. It can be a period of great uncertainty, making it necessary to identify the items of concern in order to protect both the Project Manager and his company. Project Initiation is essential to ensure a successful outcome and leads ultimately to the Baseline that was constructed in Chapter 4. Indeed, if you don't get the initiation phase right, you have no reason to expect that anything else will go right. A project never gets a second chance to make a first impression, or to correct a false start!

The checklist provides the manager with a means of ensuring that all the standard components of a project are incorporated in the planning and as many predictable sources of danger as possible are exposed before any work begins.

> ## A project never gets a second chance to make a first impression!

A successful initiation is in itself no guarantee of eventual project success, but the reverse is virtually true: a bungled initiation is almost a guarantee of project failure. The manager is warned not to accept the brief until he is satisfied that he understands what is required of him and that he has the full commitment of the organisation to which he shall report during the lifetime of the project. So the following is addressed to you, the putative project manager.

The Action Checklist

The following lengthy list of questions may not be exhaustive, as every project is different, but by asking these questions you should be able to identify whether any questions are missing. If you get every one answered to your satisfaction you will have done more than most of your predecessors towards a promising start to your project. Though I warn you, this process takes time, and your support team (and your ultimate boss) will bombard you with cries of, stop all this chatter and get on with it, to which your reply is – get on with precisely what, Sir?

Get on with what, Sir?

Existence

To what extent can the project be said to exist? Does it have a name? A number? An owner? A customer? Is it somebody's bright idea, as yet unexposed to the devils that dwell amongst the details? And if it is, is that person someone who will take criticism on board? Or will he guard his idea jealously and not be prepared to be flexible, to the extent that if the project were to fail or cease to be so would your time in the company? Or has it been thought about by people who know how to think about these things? Who are these people? To what extent are they committed to its success? Has anyone done any planning? Indeed, has anyone got as far as drawing up a Baseline and filling in the Project Initiation form (the project birth certificate)? Is there any form of tangible evidence that this project actually exists? Is it perhaps the result of a preliminary feasibility study? Or is a feasibility component required as a first phase[5]? And is there any indication of what the budget might be?

Business objectives

What are the business goals of the project? Which department in the organisation is the main beneficiary? And which department will sign off on the costs?

---

[5]   See Chapter 8 for a further discussion of feasibility studies.

Nature

What sort of project is it? What kinds of project are there? Is it a research project in which you do as much as you can within time and budget constraints, delivering a heap of paper at the end of the day? Is it a design and implementation project with a visible outcome: a building, a brochure or a ballet? Once started must it, like a bridge, be successfully completed? Or could it be abandoned if circumstances were to change, as might be the case in the design of a supersonic passenger plane which cannot meet new eco-friendly criteria? Is the intended customer internal or external to your organisation? Is it yet one more example of what we know well how to do; a copy of a series of similar predecessors, as easy as reinventing the wheel? Or is it a brave new adventure, loaded to the gunnels with risk? Could the project be jettisoned if the organisation should fall on hard times? Or might it then proceed in partnership with another organisation?

Specification

Is there a specification for the product of the project? What form does this take? A set of requirements? Engineering drawings? How detailed are they? If it is simply a rough idea, would it be your job to develop it into a detailed design as part of the project? If it is already a detailed design, has provision been made for the possibility of variations during the life of the project. Is it a cathedral, an icon to a company boss who wants to be glorified by it? Are acceptance testing, documentation and training part of the specification?

Ownership

Who is going to own the project until it is delivered to the customer? The person asking you to do the job? Is that person high enough in the organisation chart to own anything? Is he the project sponsor or champion? Politics abound in the world of the project. Who up there is going to ensure the project's continued existence? Who is going to fight your corner when budget time rolls around? Is he someone with a track record of corporate success? Or does the project not at this stage have a suitable owner?

Planning

Is there already a Baseline plan for the project? Who made it? Is your approval and acceptance of the plan allowed for in the plan itself? Are you invited to enhance it or amend it? Does the organisation have final versions of completed plans of similar projects that could be used as a starting point for the detailed Project Plan? Does the organisation use a single project planning computer system? Are you familiar with it? Or are you allowed to use any system that takes your fancy? In particular, are you required to use the British Standard PRINCE[6]?

The customer contract

We mentioned the contract already in the Introduction. This is a continuation. Is there already a customer contract, external or internal? Who has written it? The owner? The contracts department? Is it still in draft form? Or has the organisation already committed itself? Are you allowed to modify, develop, discard and restart, etc. the contract? Is it a fixed-price contract? Or is it a cost-plus project? Beware cost-plus projects, where the more the project costs, the more the contractor is paid. In cost-plus projects, cost over-runs are endemic – there is no incentive to complete the project on time and on budget. The questions to ask are: Does the contract contain penalty clauses? Does it provide for progress payments? And most important of all, is the contract contained in the body of the plan?

Is there, for example, a section in the plan entitled, Contractual Specifications, where every clause of the contract, relating to every deliverable, is referred to? If all is sweetness and light on delivery day, you can drop the plan in the company history file and just sign the contract as completed. But if in the lead up to delivery, or indeed at any time during the life of the project, there are disputes between the contracting parties, you need a document on the board room table, a corporate lens through which to peer. And there is no better document than a contract presented in plan form; enough of a plan to enable a lawyer to understand it, and enough of a contract to enable the project team to understand it. So is the contract part of the plan?

> # Is the contract part of the plan?

---

[6]   See BSI 9001 Standards

Likewise, is the plan part of the contract? Is the contract written in such a way that the planner can incorporate its essence in the plan with a minimum of potential disaster?

> ## And is the plan part of the contract?

As early as possible in the negotiation phase these two fundamental documents should be integrated. Iterating them from the stage of naïve optimism to grey-haired pessimism has the beneficial value of bringing people from both (or more than both) sides together into a dream team. As time goes on and as the potholes reveal themselves, each tribe becomes more and more eloquent in each other's speeches, relaying their understanding to their own management, paving the way for as frictionless a project atmosphere as possible. Make sure you have the inter-company arguments as much as possible during the paper stage and not at the steel-and-concrete stage.

The essential conflict between plan and contract is that if the plan doesn't precede the contract, how can you specify times and costs with any confidence? However, before you have a contract, how much are you willing to spend on the planning?

But having waded though all this discussion about contracts and plans, it must become patently clear that there is very little difference between the two, and the safest thing a company can do is include the project manager in writing (and rewriting) the contract and the negotiations (and renegotiations) between customer and supplier. An internal dispute between company management and the project manager is virtually a guarantee that the company signature is, in turn, a guarantee of successful delivery. You should consider the project manager as a sort of internal company policeman.

Acceptance procedure

The ultimate phase of the plan must be a cast-iron procedure for the two sides together to run acceptance tests. The days of the supplier leaving the product on the customer's doorstep at dead o' night are long gone. We need to know before we start how we're going to finish. We need an agreed Acceptance Document of empty boxes, together with accompanying instructions, by the start of the live project, to be morphed into a dense array of numbers, accepted by the customer at its termination. The creation of the Acceptance Document is in itself an invaluable tool of understanding between the parties. It acts as a catalyst to project thought.

In computer projects the standard names for acceptance tests are alpha (fairly primitive, quick and dirty) and beta (detailed), leading to gamma (ultimate, all-singing and dancing, please pay the lady on the way out, acceptance). As an example, the Ipswich Orwell Bridge acceptance tests consisted firstly of my doing a solo early Sunday-morning run across it and back (the successful alpha test), closely followed by a beta half-Marathon of about three hundred runners. The concrete stood up to both tests admirably, and the gamma traffic was let loose in the early afternoon, since when the bridge has functioned non-stop for thirty years.

Risk elements

Has a risk survey been carried out? If so, who are the risk owners? If not, why not and is risk analysis regarded as part of the project? Risk analysis has become a big thing in the project world, and conveys the idea that you know beforehand what all the risk elements are. To some it is meant to convey the thought that the plan doesn't contain many risky tasks. Don't let them fool you. Every single task contains risk; even the things that you've done time and time again. Trains are late, people get sick, the digging machine breaks down, someone nicks the project tea kettle. By all means subject obvious critical items to special attention, including statistical analysis of duration times; a project plan isn't a knitting pattern. But don't think that a series of successes constitutes a guarantee for future successes.

Quality and standards

In addition to your own internal, planned quality assurance regimen, what external quality standards would the project be required to satisfy? Have all Health and Safety issues been addressed? Are you familiar with them from previous experience? Which company quality organisations will be involved and are they planned for?

Budget

Has a budget been allocated to the project? Or to the work that you will need to do to complete the Project Initiation phase? How were these computed? As a result of an Outline Plan[7]? Or independently? How does the proposed budget compare with the price of the product? If it is out of kilter think long and hard as to its viability.

Reporting

To whom do you report in the organisation? What systematic reports will be required and to whom will they be sent: within the project and in the company? To the customer? By cost? By task? By WBS item? And are there procedures for specifying ad hoc reports?

Resources

Where will the project be carried out? What equipment and materials are needed? What human resources will be required? Where will they come from: home organisation v. mercenaries? Will you be allowed to select your team or will it be imposed on you? Who is responsible for making sure they turn up when needed? Remember to use the plan as your contract with each of them.

A project/programme office (see Chapter 16)

Are the services of a company Project/Programme Office available to you? What are they? Project Offices vary very widely from one-man advisors to large experienced staffs capable of carrying much of the responsibility. In particular, responsibility for planning systems, collecting hours spent, preparing reports for you – including making you aware of the critical tasks. Delegate as much as you can, but don't abdicate responsibility for any of it.

Why you?!

Why have you been chosen to lead this project? Are you the world's best in this particular field? Or are you the only one left? Have all the bright guys or those with experience already turned it down. If so why? How much project experience have you already had? Are you prepared to put in the long and anti-social hours? Do you really feel that you are the man for the

---

[7] An Outline Plan is a lightweight Baseline.

job? Or for the good of the organisation and your own career should you turn it down?

Do you really feel that you are the man for the job?

Tying in the company

If you do accept, then the last step in the initiation process is to produce the Project Initiation Document (PI),[8] a summary of the answers to the items in this chapter. Remember to obtain the signatures of the people up the line to the top, so that they are tied into the project, to be equally congratulated on the eventual success or equally culpable for the failure of the project.

And The Ultimate Question

Why don't you stop wasting time asking all these questions, and get on with it? "Get on with what, Guv?".

This check-off list comprises over 100 questions. At first sight this may seem an inordinate amount of work just to bring a project to the plan starting line; longer even than getting to the start of the London Marathon. But which of the questions could you safely ignore? Better to face the potential problems they are intended to expose than to discover them in the heat of

---

[8]   Refer back to chapter 3

battle. This is what this process sets out to achieve. Of course, you cannot hope for certainty. You don't have time. In practice only the details of the project itself can reveal all the pitfalls. But a high scoring rate at this juncture would give you grounds for optimism, while a low one would cause you to identify the usual suspects and delay the termination of the Initiation Process until both you and your management feel confident.

The next chapter ...

... introduces the role of the project owner, something strangely missing from most discussions of the nature of project management.

Chapter 8: The Project Owner

The Buck Stops Here

The sign on President Truman's desk

The Need for Ownership

Whatever the substance of a project, be it a machine of some sort, a communications network or a theatre, it will eventually be handed over to someone, its owner to be. A lot of money is about to be spent and someone has to be made responsible for that money – and everything the money is spent on. A project cannot be left to run itself, so at least it needs a manager, someone who lives with it day and night deep in the diabolical details, but even the project manager needs a friendly shoulder to weep on.

Therefore the concept of the project owner is one that we should discuss at some length. Regrettably, **ownership** of a project is very often lost in the corporate energy released at project inception and doesn't raise its head very much in the daily project turmoil. This is particularly true for governmental projects. Civil servants and ministers come and go, while the projects for which they are responsible often go on for ever, consuming considerable amounts of taxpayer money. However, it isn't easy for the taxpayer to find out how much gets spent, nor what it was spent on. Indeed this may also be true for ministers, MPs and the newspapers.

But the problem of identifying a project owner isn't restricted to public projects, it also pertains to private companies, large and small. The fundamental source of the problem in both sectors is that of visibility. Everyone knows who the project manager is. As we see time and time again in the book, the manager of a project has to be right there in the thick of it; you soon learn to recognise his voice, and his personal appearance degenerates as reality departs from the plan. But you can't see the owner. He rarely visits the vineyard and even the toilers therein may not be aware of his existence. But more to the point, he doesn't appear on the company organisation charts due to the temporary nature of the projects.

Sir! The Baseline is ready for your signature

If a project does not have a recognised owner, then the project manager clearly has no one axiomatically to report to. In turn, then, the project owner needs to have someone to report to. But who should this be? The CEO? The chairman of the board? The Cabinet? A committee of some sort? And what are his duties and responsibilities? When you say he is the owner, is he the owner in the sense of your owning your lawn mower? Is it **his** money on the line? Is he required to stay it out until the project is over? Can you stop him leaving the company? Suppose the CEO can't find anyone to do the owning, must he do the owning himself? As well as run the company? Perhaps the inability of finding an owner is a valuable litmus test of the project's validity. If you can't find someone who believes in it there is probably a good reason; it could be that there is nothing really there to believe in.

> ## At the very minimum, the Project Owner should sign off the Baseline

Minimum Required Input

The project owner is the person whose door is permanently open to the project manager. He is the person with whom the manager discusses all unanticipated, unplanned problems, and who takes executive action to ensure solutions. In large companies with large projects he may have just one project to manage as in the case, say, of manufacturing an aircraft. With smaller projects the project owner may have other work items to undertake and this activity, while of top priority, is in practice part-time.

In both instances, the project owner should be keeping in constant touch with the project manager, smoothing his path, checking on progress to be sure that all is being done as it should and that all the necessary resources are being put at the project manager's disposal.

The project owner will have an understanding of the corporate (or public sector) strategy and the financial and resource constraints within which the project operates.

The project owner should decide what reports are required on a day-to-day or periodic basis in order to monitor the progress of the project. Theirs is an enabling role to facilitate the project manger and to champion his efforts at the corporate level. They are responsible for making sure the necessary resources are made available so that the project manager can successfully do his job.

The project owner will also be responsible for the financial accountability and risk management aspects of the project.

Accounting Framework

Hovering over every project is the collection of laws relating to finance and accounting. Now the chances are that the project manager is not from the finance department. He must of course be fully aware of the financial implications of the project, task by task and component by component. He must arrange for the plan to follow progress at short enough intervals to be able to rescue sudden departures from its current version, reporting clearly to everyone involved. On the other hand his attention should not be distracted from the current work by legal or senior managerial requirements for cost reporting. Top level corporate fiscal surveillance has to be one of the prime responsibilities of the project owner, which means that he should be conversant with the accounting laws.

In the first instance, it is the role of the project owner to provide the required information on the state of the project. In practice, this will then be signed off by the board of directors for the company's accounts.

The accountability of the project owner is a significant determinant of the success or failure of the project. In the private sector the majority of companies involved in major projects are public companies. The board of directors is accountable to its shareholders and each quarter or half year figures are posted to the stock exchange on which their shares are listed.

These figures relate to both historic performance and to future guidance. The directors and their company's performance are subject to the scrutiny of investment analysts and fund managers.

In the world of public companies there is an established regimen of accounting rules and risk management procedures. Projects that have an impact on a company's performance will be subject to periodic financial review and a variety of risk assessment techniques, including Sensitivity Analysis, Scenarios and Simulation. The object of the exercise is to gain an understanding of the risk profile of the project as it evolves and to keep a close eye on how any downside risks are evolving.

There is a wide literature on risk management techniques, which differentiate risk and uncertainty. Risk is quantifiable to some degree in probabilistic terms while uncertainty is unquantifiable. A prudent project manager should acquaint himself with the financial framework under which his project owners operate.

Perhaps it is not surprising to find that it is in the public sector, where the financial reporting and accountability framework is limited, that there are project management graveyards galore (see Chapter 20).

Conclusion

One possible candidate for ownership is the originator of the project. He might have convinced the company of its viability and has therefore become the budget getter, while one of his responsibilities might be the customer calmer. The owner needs to be fully conversant with the physical nature of the project, the contract that gives the project life, the order of magnitude of its cost and the latest estimates of the project duration. But he will almost certainly not get into the details of its implementation. Though not all chapters of the book will be of absorbing interest, the owners should nevertheless know what they contain. However, the owner will inevitably be in close contact with the project manager to seek specific detail, as required, and can use these chapters to get hold of simple background explanations of the main strands of project flow. Let the book tell you what the questions are.

The next chapter ....

... gets you from the primeval glimmerings to the substantial organisation and from impossibility to the almost possible. The Big Bong. Paper plan. Substantial plan. Budget. Team. Spectral position. Turmoil. Tie-in with this chapter. Big Bong 2. Project organisation chart.

Chapter 9: Coping With the Run Up

Many shall run to and fro, and knowledge shall be increased

Daniel 12, verse 4

Introduction

This chapter is aimed primarily at the Project Manager. However, I have tried to make it as broad, interesting and readable as possible so everyone involved can read it.

Projects never start and having started never finish, as many a project person will tell you. But what's so special about projects? Well, *Homo sapiens* lives in a soup of ideas, each vying for attention: shoes and ships and sealing wax, cabbages and kings and mobile phones... Somehow, we have to decide which of these things we should make and how to make them. So how and where do we start? Just about everything seems to have a primary cause, except perhaps the Big Bang. But are you even sure of that?

> **There is a fascinating similarity between the initiation of the universe and that of a project**

The hydrogen atoms of the Big Bang weren't the fundamental particles of creation. It seems that we already had the quarks, leptons, baryons, mesons, etc and now the Higg's Boson and even they may turn out to be unfundamental as science peers ever more deeply into matter and beyond today's visible horizon. A lot of things must have happened before our time zero. There might even have been an infinite amount of negative, pre-bang time for all we yet know. We may well be living in an eternal project that never actually started, so why should we be surprised to learn that simpler projects are substantially different? There is a fascinating similarity between the initiation of the universe and that of a project.

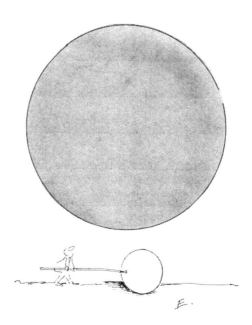

At the start the task may look impossible

Where does it all begin, then? Why a new ship? Because of changes in transportation economics? New tourist sites? Discoveries of cleaner types of fuel requiring new propulsion units? Or because the whim of the captain's girl friend, who has just read about a Quinquireme of Ninevah? But even as I wrote those words I had the sudden idea of returning to the age of sail for bulk, non-deteriorating goods to eliminate the cost of fuel. Or perhaps reopening the canals. But what would I have to do to take the idea beyond that of idle dreaming between sentences? Whom should I talk to? A transportation consultant? A model builder? A retired sea dog? How do you get an idea going? And at what point can it be considered to be more than just an idea? When I've paid someone to do something? But what should that something be? And how much would it cost me? And to what extent do I own the idea? Can you, in fact, own ideas? Before you patent them? And who can you trust once the idea is out? And so on and so on.

But even in writing these words I might have initiated a project. Someone with more vision than I might seize upon it and in some years time produce the Millenniumship, get rich and buy me a lunch. When might he say the project started? So it isn't easy, but you have at some point to say that you have a tangible entity on your hands that is no longer just pure whimsy.

The fact is that there is rarely an objective moment when a project tells you that it has started. You have to do this yourself, and probably the best time would be the time when serous money gets involved. But how serious is serious? Only you can know that. But it could coincide with the point at which three people are involved, say. Or when you set up a separate bank account. Or when you dedicate an office with the project name on the door. Or when the project name appears on the computerised planning list. Or when a salesman barges in and blocks your doorway. Or when your kids no longer recognise you. OK, this list is endless. But at some stage, either you put the idea out of your head or it takes up residence.

Enter the Big Bong

So starting a project is like creating the universe, so what you should do is have a mini Big Bang, ***Old Norman's "Big Bong"***. You install a large brass gong just outside your office, keeping the bong banger in a locked drawer.

The impossible about to start

Then when you have decided that seriousness has descended you go out and strike the gong, announcing to your little world that a series of pre-projects is to be created; a cloud of primitive corporate hydrogen awaits some gravity to coalesce into everything this book is about. And the best way, indeed the only way, is to evolve it in the following careful steps:-

The Big Bong

The paper plan

Now don't start off by digging anything, or hammering anything or buying anything – except for some pads of paper. Start by talking, shouting, gesticulating and drawing on the white board. Perhaps for a whole day or even an entire weekend. Then start writing it down, and have someone write it up to be distributed the next day.

> **It will have produced a veritable cloud of corporate hydrogen**

You might consider including a professional planner right from the start to crystallise the discussion, to the extent that he understands it. But it could perhaps well be a waste of time yet; let the tangible outcome be reams of paper, leading eventually to a Plan.

If this process evolves into an entire week it will have produced a veritable cloud of corporate hydrogen – but it will have cost the company little more than battered egos. Then there should be a pause for reflection (and possible amnesia), to be followed a month later by a further and more formal round. Then a possible third round, involving a higher level of participation, including someone with the authority to spend money.

If by the end of this proto project there is a feeling of optimism amongst the proto team then you probably have something viable on your hands. It will have a working name, though probably not yet a number. Someone of fairly senior standing will probably have begun to feel a sense of ownership of it and a sense of excitement will have begun to pervade the corporate atmosphere. But little more can be said at this abstract level – except for one very serious question: is there anything of an experimental nature involved in the discussion so far? If so, drop all else and make the decision, one way or the other, either to carry out the experiment alone or do nothing at all.

The fundamental problem with experiments is that they are always successful – if carried out properly. Properly conducted experiments always tell you something – though possibly not what you had hoped for. There is absolutely no point in attaching anything of substantial importance to a project component that you cannot guarantee will work and that cannot be reasonably estimated in terms of time and cost. By all means carry out experiments, but don't bet your company or its reputation on them; you don't want a Bristol Brabazon aeroplane or a Deepwater Horizon platform on your hands.

The feasibility study

So, once you have a paper plan that has stood the test of several iterations with little important change from one to another, you may feel ready to embark on the real thing. But don't jump the gun. Ask the question whether the paper plan contains any potential research elements; any possible saboteurs. If so, identify the three most vulnerable and make each the subject of a feasibility mini-project. This will probably need the purchase of materials and equipment, and will certainly need people. But be prepared to spend the money. It will enable you to defend the decision to spend significantly more should the main project get a go-ahead. In particular, if the uncertainty is that of time estimates, computer time is cheap these days. Let the computer run all night testing ranges of time estimates, displaying distribution curves – from shortest to longest, as well as most probable. Statistical computer runs don't guarantee anything, but staring at plotted results can give you a warm feeling – or a cold one – and hopefully increase your faith to the extent of going for the substantial plan. At least thereafter you can assume that miss-matches between plan and reality will be minor ones.

The substantial plan

So you've succeeded in convincing enough colleagues of the viability of the idea: at least enough to obtain some money. You are far yet from being able to estimate a full-blown programme of work, but at least you know what you need to know to do this, and how to get to that point. So you're initiating a pre-project, or even the first in a series of pre-projects leading hopefully to a full go-ahead. And the time has come to stop all that scribbling and instead to cover the floor in aluminium chips.

No early Egyptian ever rode in a chariot

Now is the time to assign engineers and draughtsmen to professional drawings to replace the rough sketches. You may need to bring in model makers to build models for testing and as a means of conveying your ideas. But beware the terrible curse placed on models from the dawn of man; models don't scale up easily. The very early Egyptians had the wheel as a toy, but it wasn't until the Middle Kingdom that they managed to scale it up to build the chariot, overcoming the large scale axle friction problem.

The first act of the substantial plan must be the final act of the paper plan repeated in much greater detail. You will need five[9] people to carry out

---

[9] Experience shows that five people is the optimal group size for getting things done. More than five means the start of writing things down on paper between the group members; the beginning of bureaucracy. Beyond five, the amount of time writing memos within the group increases rapidly, reducing creative work and initiating a command and control structure, which inhibits the creative process. Less than five may leave gaps in the expertise required.

these initial tasks as well as the tasks that will inevitably be discovered and planned while the initial tasks are being worked on. And to give yourself a goal, as arbitrary as it may be, plan to have a milestone three months away – and stick to it. Call it a Feasibility Review – and stick to it. Book the room immediately – and stick to the date. Invite an independent review team of knowledgeable people: employees or even friendly competitors, but with the probable exception of the customer – though see below. Let each phase of the plan be preceded by a modicum of ceremony and ended with a serious review – including the deliberate decision to continue or stop. A healthy company is a company in which stopping projects is an understood and accepted part of corporate life. If the truth were known, in the world of both business and government far too much money is spent chasing bad projects which turn into terrible investments.

At the root of the problem lies *Old Norman's Law of Inverse Momentum*: the probability of stopping a non-starter is inversely proportional to how long ago it actually started; the more you have spent on the run-up the more difficult it is to stop further spending. The irony here is that the more you have spent the more obvious it has become that it has been misspent, but the more you have spent the more petrified the company becomes in admitting the fact: it takes a very strong boss to stand up and admit defeat. But it isn't defeat. What's spent is spent; it is a sunk cost. There's nothing you can do about it – instead, profit from what you have learnt from the spending.

And out of disaster can come unthought of roses of success. In the early 1960s IBM had spent a fortune developing and building their 8000-series of computers, a modest improvement on the earlier 7000-series. But on the night before its global announcement Tom Watson, the IBM President, cancelled it and sent the project team back to the drawing boards. Admittedly, few companies at that time had the resources to do such a thing, and IBM had to survive on rejigged earlier computers to calm Boeing down, as well as the rest of their customer base. But the decision led to the announcement of the 360-series in 1964, with the birth of the byte and much else that became fundamental to the further evolution of the computer.

The fact that you might look a bit frazzled on a review day must not deter you. If you delay the review day once you can do it again – and even again, and the delays will become worse than the events you are trying to suppress. On the other hand, your invited guests should be the very people you need to help you. Turn it round and make the milestones pleas for help rather than statements of success.

The plan will grow day by day as new discoveries are made, and what you do each day will be a combination of what you had planned earlier plus building on yesterday's discoveries. And included in the plan will be ideas for the removal of tasks as you discover that earlier ideas are no longer viable, to be replaced by later ones. Remember, part of the value of starting a project is discovering what the project is and learning how to do it. At this early stage the plan has to be a living, breathing evolving animal, a sort of cross between a tiger and a jellyfish.

At the start, the plan will be very simple and will bear little resemblance to versions further down the line, but there's a vast difference between a simple plan and no plan at all. No plan means no catalyst, no structured discussions out there in the corridor.

The budget

There is very little you can do about pre-Bong expenditure. You can try to remember what you've already done and write yourself a number on a piece of paper, or you might actually have a standing pre-project budget from which you might have helped yourself. But this is not very important. At this early stage rather amateur activity costs are comparatively small compared with what's to follow. What is important now is to charge everything you spend. But charge it to what? Ah, this is the point at which you should set up a budget. Later on, budgets will become complicated but at least they will arrive automatically – one of the great benefits of the planning system. But right now you can easily create a budget dedicated to the project simply by saying so in the nascent plan. Assume the cost of five people, full time for three months: £75,000 say. Give it a number, freeze it, proclaim it on the wall just by your desk and hand out a simple form to the five participants – as well as yourself. But place an A4 box of forms where everyone can see it so that anybody you hadn't thought of at the start can join in and write down their hours.

Now the budget at this stage has nothing to do with the Payroll System. No real money will be charged against it, but the costs of the hours are there to be added later to the project actual costs – for corporate profitability calculations and corporate learning purposes. But be warned. After three months you may well have accumulated a paper cost of twice your original estimate. This will be a sobering discovery and will accelerate your efforts to get the project accepted at higher levels and properly funded.

The team

At this early stage, who are you? You can be just anyone. Anybody can have ideas; anybody can discover or invent things. The idea of the project could be yours, but you may well not be the eventual project manager; you could have a clear idea of what you'd like to have done, but not have enough experience or self-confidence to see how to do it. There is nothing wrong in that.

> ## Or your grandmother might have asked you where you supposed she got her money

You could be the owner, but if you were a bankrupt inventor who had sweet-talked an investor, the latter may have wrested any potential ownership from you. Likewise, you may have gone to a lawyer at an early stage to shore up your defences, and he might have scared you into letting him have some ownership as the price for writing tough contracts. Or your grandmother might have asked you where you supposed she got her money from.

Moreover, a fledgling project may pass quite rapidly through a variety of phases until it settles down into a recognisable entity. At each phase there might be different, perhaps short-lived, groups of specialists working on a series of possible sabotaging problems until the project had crystallised itself out into its main lines of development.

And don't ignore possible customers. They could tell you very early on that no one wants a digital clotheshorse. Invite an occasional friendly customer to a presentation and save yourself some money.

Its spectral position

You can classify a project into one of any range of candidates: large or small, cheap or expensive, a brand new idea – even a piece of research – or number one thousand and one of an ancient series. You might be designing a pneumatic vehicle to reduce city noise and pollution or you might be building yet another bridge, choreographing a ballet or preparing a new atlas. You may be working towards a contracted deliverable, threatened by a jungle of penalty clauses, or you may be working in splendid isolation in a hollowed-out log while the world gets on with its business, oblivious of the miracle to be foisted upon them, with your grandmother searching for you in the woods. But whatever it is don't waste time discussing it. Just get on with it.

The turmoil

The bulk of the talking, shouting, drawing, experimenting, writing, etc. as the essence of the project evolves, will take place very much at random: in random places and between random people. This is the best way to start anything. You throw out ideas and you see what happens to them. To you the ideas were good – otherwise we wouldn't be here. But if they are good they will dominate the activity, and righteousness will prevail. It will become a paper-intensive exercise as ideas are fought over, but with time someone will start writing dates on the sheets and you'll know that reality is starting to emerge, and with dates, titles, and with titles, language – the nouns and the verbs of a plan. Time to find a planner.

The planner

You can make a good start without actually employing the services of an experienced planner. Things are so simple that you can write or draw the plan yourself, you don't need a computer yet. However, in addition perhaps to advising you to consider chatting up a possible source of economic help and bending the ear of a friendly lawyer, what I would very strongly recommend is the early services of a planner, at least on a part-time basis, even though you may think it a bit of an economic burden. Professional planners have been through it all before. They ask questions, and a large part of their value is trying to force answers out of you; planners keep you on the straight and narrow. Rectilinearity and eyes of needles are in very short supply during the early phases of a project, but an experienced planner can quickly straighten and shorten your path simply by refusing to understand what you are up to. The secret of General Sherman's success was that he kept a planner chained up just outside his tent. In addition to having to understand the plan, the planner had to explain it to the other generals. The theory was that if he could understand it, even generals could understand it.

> **Eyes of needles are in very short supply**

But not only will the planner prise decisions from you and catalyse the project's forward movement, if he hangs copies of the latest versions on the wall he will create an atmosphere of creativity in your vicinity and will impress possible visitors, not least potential customers, that all is well in hand. People don't have to read it, and probably wouldn't be able to anyway, but its existence would make an unforgettable impression on entering the room.

Chapter 7 consisted of a long list of questions that need to be answered before a manager dare accept the brief of running a project. Now there's no way of answering those questions without having done a lot of digging into detail, and the best way of doing so, instead of sitting around a large room on day minus one, is to evolve the answers as you follow the route described herein. You should use this section as your map, oscillating back and forth until someone gives the Bong two bangs. The two together form an iterative process that will enable you to hit the deck running.

Big Bong Two

If you get this far and if each of three, say, three-monthly reviews has been an honest battle between those who hold the purse strings and those with the scissors, then a project will have emerged, the first phase of which could well be some corporate sessions with likely customers. Customers can be a free source of competence. Listen to them. Boeing knew far more about using computers than IBM did, and produced some world-beating software that IBM could never have imagined. But at the same time, since Lufthansa was the only customer on the horizon when the 737 reached this stage, Lufthansa's design influence was substantial. And what an unrivalled success it became; the jet age successor to the DC 3 Dakota.

So, although projects are theoretically impossible, we have evolved ourselves into one anyway, and the time has come to create an appropriate (though temporary) structure. In fact, we need a POC, a Project Organisation Chart, comprising all the functional bodies described so far in this book. And a good place to put it temporarily is the top right hand corner of the (permanent) Company Organisation Chart. We need:-

A Project Owner: a senior manager, who must appear on a quasi-permanent Company Organisation Chart. He's a Janus: his ultimate responsibility is to be the face of the company to the project team and the face of the project to the company management. He must have the same feeling of ownership towards the project as he does towards his house, his car or his football team. He must care for it as he cares for his garden. He must nourish the team members as he nourishes his family. And he must believe in the project as he believes in another tomorrow; he may need those tomorrows.

A Project Manager: a person whose working life shall be devoted to running the project with tenacity and to the exclusion of all other company responsibilities. Preferably, it should be someone who has recently emerged from a successful project and preferably a similar one. But such people are difficult to find, most of them are still inaccessible on other projects. But though project managers don't grow on trees, there are plenty of technical people who have learnt a lot about management during their project career and who could make a good stand-in. He will need a bit of assistance from on high – and from the team. But this is the way all project managers are made, as we all know. In some ways a previous assistant project manager who has just emerged from the fray could be an excellent choice. He will want to prove himself and may have fresh memories of how not to do things, culled from previous experience. There is however one important prerequisite, experience of projects.

Task Managers: we introduced the possible need for Task Managers in Chapter 6. It is advisable to list the manager of each task of long duration.

A Planner: someone with solid experience of planning. If available, either a fully-fledged planner or an erstwhile assistant planner eager to take on the major role. Essentially all project planning is done on computers and a rich source of experienced planners is the computer industry itself. Indeed, a good argument can be made for recruiting planners from outside the engineering professions. Perhaps too much specialisation in the electrical profession could make it difficult for an electrical engineer to understand a mechanical engineer. One of the problems almost unique to projects is the language problem.[10] It might be better to hire a technical writer or scientific author as a trainee planner: someone used to a wide range of jargon. Bletchley Park wasn't staffed by many professional code-breakers; but by crossword solvers, chess players and highly numerate people generally.

A Project Secretary: Someone who knows what's supposed to be happening and acts for the project manager when possible or alerts him when necessary. This person should have as little scheduled work as possible, allowing them freedom to wander around as circumstances permit or require.

The piping chap couldn't change a light bulb

Evolving the one into the other: the ultimate goal is to let the Project Organisation Chart evolve into the company chart for the duration of the project. If you were to achieve this you would have the making of a super-efficient company.[11]

The next chapter ...

... is about coping with the reality of the project. Day Zero. Codes. Hours worked. Costs. The two terminal meetings. The diary. The back office.

---

[10] As described later in chapters 12 and 14
[11] See chapter 14 for some ideas.

Chapter 10: Coping With Reality – Enter the Project Owner

Between the idea and the reality falls the shadow

T. S. Eliot

Why Isn't Something Happening?

This chapter describes the owner's responsibilities on the first day of a project, and later brings in the project manager, at which point, for a while, their roles become indistinguishable. The Big Day has arrived and the project is finally a living, breathing thing – except that you, the project owner, can't hear much breathing. Why not? Be it known that the first day of any live project is called Day Zero. The reason for this is that it is the first day in the life of the project, but it is a day on which nothing creative happens. There may be other non-productive days, but this is the first one and there may be many explanations. But of all the explanations, perhaps the most telling is that none of the technical members of the team is yet available; they are still working on their previous project. They said they'd be ready. They thought they'd be ready. They hoped they'd be ready, but at the last moment they realised that their time-estimate was (yet again) optimistic. You are the project owner, nevertheless, be warned, you can expect an all-pervading silence to reign – except for the noise you are invited to make by visiting the site and making yourself known by helping the secretary find a desk, a telephone, a computer, some printer paper and ink. Just being there will set the tone for the project that only you can achieve. Take along your toolbox and fix the coat hanger to the wall. Think how best to make your presence appreciated.

> **None of the technical members of the team is yet available.**

Have a talk with the project manager and help him ring around the organisations who are supposed to be supplying the team members. Ask to see their expectant empty desks. Make sure the latest version of the project plan is up on everybody's screen, or blu-tacked to the wall, and that the project planner is on his way; it won't be long before he will start making modifications – though hopefully very minor ones.

In short, do everything you can to have a reception committee ready and waiting for the first arrivals, even though it may consist of little more than you, the project manager and the secretary. Greet everyone upon their arrival and ensure that the project team knows who you are. They may well not see you every day of this project, but they need to know that there is someone from the Head Shed who cares about them and the project – and they have someone to whom they may turn in their hour of need. They need to be told that this is the most important programme of work in which this company is engaged. They need to know that their presence is vital to its success and that they are valued members of the team, that management will be watching their progress matched against their commitments and your expectations. You might also have to introduce them to the project manager if he is running late elsewhere. Also make sure that they know how to report the start and finish dates of the tasks they are working on, how the documentation process works, their hours of work and what to do should they begin to realise that a task is going to overrun its estimated duration.

> ## There, I've written your speech of welcome for you

The Project Manager's Day Zero

At this point we turn to the project manager. Day Zero will be a most frustrating day for you, too. You have perhaps several planned tasks to get moving – by definition, at least one. You will have made screen or printed versions of these available to the people involved. When they show up you will also explain to them the importance of their timely reporting the number of hours worked on each task to your screen. Each task will start at the first instance of work being charged to it, but will finish when you say so, at which point you will put the barrier up preventing anyone charging to it; if they insist on so doing you will learn something about the task and another chunk of the contingency reserve will have been used.

The resource codes were entered into the task data at planning time, and specific names shortly before they are required, as shown in the diagram:-

TASK NAME									
DU	ID	ES	EF	LS	LF	Bill	Fred	Wheelbarrow	Shovel

So you know who and what are supposed to be there.

Hours Worked

Taking hours worked as an example, it is important always to have in mind the inestimable value to the company of the eventual feeding-forward of experience gained from this project to the next. As we said earlier, not all worked hours may be paid hours. For project accounting purposes, hours worked must be reported in full to the system to produce an accurate version of reality, with which to compare the original estimates. The planner needs to know at the end of the day how accurate the planning was, and will be able to use this project's actual data as estimates for the next similar project's planning process. However, not all worked hours may be paid for, depending on corporate policy. Work performed outside standard working time, for example, late evenings and weekends, although possibly inadmissible for payroll purposes, should be registered for project purposes.

The raw hour data should be entered just the once and migrated to both the project and the payroll systems, (each possibly provided by two different companies). That's a management decision. Care must therefore be taken to distinguish between the two as data is passed between them.

The labour cost of the task can be the product of the number of hours, independent of people's names, using a single average hourly rate. This is usually good enough. For project purposes it isn't necessary to include individual hourly rates – which change from time to time. Moreover, at the Come to God and Spreading the Gospel meetings at the end of the project (see below) a typical question of pure absorption will be, how did the actual hours spent compare with the estimates? So the project manager's focus is on hours worked, not the cost of the hours. The latter is for others to decide.

Then there are the non-human resources, the rented equipment, the premises, and the equipment brought in just for the project. These are all specified at planning time and have to be registered when they arrive on the job. This might well involve an inspection at the Goods Inwards bay, remote from the project management office, typical of much project work. Indeed work performed on the project may well be spread over a wide geographic area, requiring as much automatic data transmission as possible to make the management as seamless and fluent as possible.

Other Cost Information

In addition to the hours worked and the costs thereof, we have the arrival of ordered tools, parts and equipment, initiating the receivable documents and payments, rentals for hired equipment and premises, et cetera. Each item is entered into the planning system, as described in Chapter 11. The output will be reports sent to the project manager and whoever else requires them. This leads ultimately to the total story of the project and to its place in the history of the company. The first step in this history is to hold a couple of post-project meetings, or, as I call them, the "Come to God" and "Spreading the Gospel" meetings. The importance of which receives little prominence in the project press. However, they are invaluable.

The Come to God Meeting

At this point I will leap over everything to warn you about what you'll have to do immediately the project is over. I do this to give you the ultimate reason for focussing your thoughts on the need for the accurate reporting, which is the crux of this chapter.

Looking forward, then, to day one of post-project life, you should organise and run two meetings, the first, as mentioned above, is the Come to God meeting. All those tightly involved with the project attend this meeting plus company people, as high up as you can persuade to come, hired hands, customers — including their MDs — and consultants if you've needed them. The lists include all who have primarily contributed to the successes of the project, including those who have rescued it from disaster — as well as those who caused the disasters.

> **Nothing like raw material from the trenches for entertaining those at the meeting**

Everyone shall be issued a copy of the initial version of the Baseline, material updates and the final version of the plan as actually carried out. You probably won't want to bury them in the entirety of the documentation, but you should make it possible to access documents via the screens strategically arrayed around the room. Of the documentation the most important for the purposes of the meeting will be the notes written on the fly in the heat of battle; nothing like the raw material from the trenches for entertaining those at the meeting.

The dress code for the meeting is jackets and ties off, and there in no seating plan. The primary purpose of the meeting is to help those involved and the organisation do a better job next time. Reputations should be built on making new mistakes at every turn, and not repeating the old ones.

You, the project manager, remind those at the meeting of what we did: those breakfasts with Proctor and Gamble, the way Fred got the cement delivered on time despite the truck drivers' strike, how we unrolled the entire plan on the table in the Japanese MD's office and returned three days later to be awarded the contract despite our price and the power cut in the middle of the presentation. Let jollity reign; old enmities transformed now into lifelong amity; personal networks extended. If you haven't yet experienced this jamboree you've got a nice surprise in store. It has to be experienced to be believed.

All followed by a long-awaited liquid lunch. Believe me, this is a magic meeting; the jewel in the crown of any project.

The Spreading the Gospel Meeting

Then comes the after-life, post-project day 2, the internal meeting with teams from the company's other projects. Same room, some of the same people, including those from the head office. The difference is you are replacing the outsiders with company people on other live projects. They've been too busy to watch you at work, and they're probably too busy to show up, so kidnap them. They and you will be glad you did so by the time the meeting is over.

Again, everyone is issued with a copy of the Baseline and final versions of the plan. You give a brief overview of what happened throughout its life, followed by presentations by key players: maximum one hour total.

And award yourself a medal

You then throw the meeting over to the visiting teams, inviting their questions, critiques, and utterances of disbelief of the fact that the customer actually paid and has started to discuss their follow-on contractual proposals. The key to an exciting meeting is to dwell mainly on the problems and their solutions, not on the smooth running. (If there was any smooth running, just display the corresponding sections of the plan, Baseline and Actual, and award yourself a medal.)

As in the previous meeting, make sure the project owner and his cronies are present. They will find these sessions far more instructive than board meetings.

Companies are not universities

In Chapter 14 we talk about the many uses of the Project Plan – probably much more than might strike the unaccustomed eye – it concludes with a section on corporate learning, a vastly underestimated activity. These Come to God and Spreading the Gospel meetings should be regarded as an essential part of your company's culture and intrinsic value. Too many companies allow departmental independence to repeat their mistakes. Companies are not universities; there is no equivalent of academic freedom. Feedback, analysis and learning from mistakes and successes save money and improve a company's wherewithal to compete (and stay in business).

Keeping a Diary

After a look at the end of the project to bring home the importance of what we are discussing, we are now back to its beginning and the importance of keeping a diary.

In addition to hours worked each day, you also need to keep a diary of what was done in those hours. This is done by means of a task message facility, each task having a Task Information button containing a Notes field. As project manager you may write as many notes per task as you like. The more the merrier, time permitting. Then at report time, all you have to do is press the Print Notes button to disgorge acres of explanations in which to bury and impress the Important People. Indeed, as the days passed you should be writing a to-do list and a diary. At the end of it all you would also be reminding yourself of the microscopic problems that conspired to sabotage the whole caboodle as you went along. En route you should send task-by-task e-mails to inform key people of the progress or lack of it, with brief explanations[12].

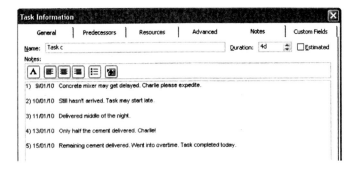

Task Information: diary page.

---

[12]   See chapter 14 to see how this is done.

The Back Office

Perhaps buried in the fine print of the Plan are the items of legal interest. Lawyers may not be explicitly named in the tasks, but will certainly be there in both spirit and letter, and should be watching progress like hawks. However, lawyers are but one part of the Back Office. Others will include the company people who might be engaged in one way and another on the project, though not mentioned explicitly in task data: drivers, accountants, stock keepers, copier operators, internal mail deliverers, etc.

Collecting Back Office data is a problem that must be solved and there are several ways of doing it. The difficult way is to have each participant report their hours per task. The issue here is that their time could be so fractionated that it would be difficult to keep tabs on which project they were working on from moment to moment, and the time taken to report the time could exceed the time to be reported. The better way is to use a formula to apportion the overheads evenly over the project as each is carried out. Even better would be to report the high earners individually and the not-so-high as overheads. This is clearly a local decision, and people need to know where they fit into the scheme of things.

The next chapter ...

... is about the reporting progress. Types of report. Actuals v. Baseline. Add-on features. Resource requirements. Capacity. Milestone tracking. Costs. Client reports.

Chapter 11: Reporting Progress

> *Progress is a comfortable disease.*
>
> e. e. cummings

Beyond Day Zero

We have now arrived at a weak point in any project, that of getting people to tell the project manager what they are doing. Once things have started, this is the project manager's primary occupation and greatest headache. During the run up and the planning he should do everything he can to automate the reporting function. He is of much greater value getting physical things done rather than dashing around handing out pens to people, or showing them how to use a keyboard.

This chapter is another one for the project manager. It is about optimising the reporting progress within your company, opening it up to a wide variety of interested parties, either working on the project or profoundly connected to it. You have planned everything down to the minutest task, work has actually started, trenches are being dug and cables laid, people are reporting their hours, paid or not, equipment is arriving, Actual Starts and even Actual Finishes are being reported. The project exists. But how's it all progressing? You should be able to find out what tasks, if any, have become critical since yesterday and you have probably been able to leap on your bike to find out what to do about it. You might have been able to deal with a smallish number of critical problems of an emergency nature.

But the question is, how's it all going? People who ask this kind of question aren't the sort of people who get terribly excited about individual, and usually temporary, problems and your reply is simply, on schedule, x days behind or x days ahead of schedule. They just seek an A-OK answer (that the situation couldn't be any better). They want to be assured that there are no problems. Everything is going to plan. Roll on that day! If there was anything they could do to help they should volunteer their services. However, in the main, they are the people whom you wouldn't dare invite to a serious discussion of the devil dwelling in the details. But all projects have them. Project management is all about flushing out problems and solving them. The only people you want to talk to about specifics are the people living intimately with what is going on – while they on the other hand have little interest in the total picture, and are unlikely to possess the ability to handle it.

Projects are like war. War is fought by groups of ten soldiers or fewer, even down to individuals. They know intimately what's expected of them, though much of it may not get reported. Somehow, the actions of the few get integrated up the line into the blurred actions of the many, and ultimately to the national level at which point little of the detail is either sought or made available. But there is a difference. War is not a contractual operation. Its owner, if it can be said to have one, is the public, the nation on whose behalf the war is being carried out. But the general populace are of least concern. They are the least consulted in the first place and last to know at the end of the day. Their only influence consists in their being a large number; they have an eventual vote, but that might be a long way off.

Breakfasts with Procter and Gamble are now thankfully in an irretrievable past

---

In the project world, although individual actions may be of heroic importance (nobody told me that the supplier closed up at five o'clock so I forced his lock and nicked the pipes; we had them all installed and running before first shift showed up; please buy the supplier a new lock), we don't hand out medals. But we do need to have some sort of picture of how it's all going, if for no other reason than that the customer is of an inevitably suspicious nature, lacking any humanity. (My memories of working breakfasts with Procter and Gamble, a bar of whose soap can be found at every sink in my house, are now thankfully in an irretrievable past. But my erstwhile friends at P&G were very nice people.)

There are very good internal reasons, of course, why we need to know. Are we over-running the budget? Are our man-hour estimates being adhered to? Are our suppliers supplying? Are our deadlines dying? And, don't forget, there's a queue of other projects out there hoping to start when the current team has completed this one.

Coping With the Limited PC Screen Size

From Chapter 3 onwards we discussed the multiplicity of information fields that comprise the standard planning systems and it is of course these fields that we use to report progress. In principle, we can bring up and print out any fields we like, at any point in time, but in practice, messing around with fields on the fly is time-consuming and frustrating. Much better to decide at the start what information we need on a regular basis, and have it portrayed in the most assimilable way, as pictorially possible. Let your planning system provide the raw data, but have a set of add-on systems, specified by you, that arrange the data you routinely require in a way that suits you best.

Life is always hoping there will be a next time

Add-on Facilities

As we noted in Chapter 6 there are specialist companies who supply fundamental software that becomes a de facto part of your planning software. They also provide corresponding reporting facilities.

**Life is always hoping that
there will be a next time**

Typical global reports obtainable from the suppliers are as follows:-

Capacity: Comparisons of planned work with skills capacity to highlight bottlenecks and underutilisation. To help us know answers to such questions as: should we be hunting for extra staff, for alternative suppliers, or do we have too many people, or have an uneven distribution of specialists?

Work carried out: Here you have to decide whether to distinguish between total hours and paid hours, remembering that from the project point of view you need to know the total effort a task took, not just the paid effort. Life is always hoping that there will be a next time.

Process discipline: Are you running a tight enough ship? Are the timesheets arriving on time and in the right place? Are the backroom boys telling you what they're doing for you?

Milestone tracking: In Chapter 4, we discussed plan structure: how to start at the top and drill down to a level at which the tasks are fairly uniform and uncomplicated. At the top level the plan should cover each major component of the project's deliverables, to include, say, the work to be done by an individual department. With such a structure there will typically be an owner; somebody to whom their component is a project in its own right. At the top level we call such segments milestones (millstones at the working level). Each milestone owner should watch his component with avid interest to ensure a blameless life, innocent of all criticality.

Costs: The ultimate goal of the project is to deliver something, and this has to be done as close to the final deadline as possible. But in practice, you may well find out that it is the cost of the whole caboodle that interests most of your audience. Often costs are easier to talk about than physical objects. Nevertheless, an interesting fact about projects that you rarely hear about is that after the dust has settled the cost problems are forgotten. The Sydney Opera House cost an estimated seventeen times what the architect said, but it has become the Eiffel Tower of Sydney. Indeed, if we look closely enough at the facts of life, we find a plethora of permanent structures, which were uneconomical until the economics were forgotten; perhaps project evolution is intrinsically un-Darwinian. Perhaps one of the few major historical examples of economically successful projects is the collection of museums, etc. masterminded by Prince Albert resulting from the Great Exhibition in the mid-nineteenth century. However, you cannot take much comfort from such philosophy; while society may honour your achievements in later life, you may pay dearly at the time for the cost overrun of implementing them. You need to have actual cost versus estimated cost on a short lead.

> **Almost everything of a permanent nature is uneconomical until the economics are forgotten**

General comparisons: The cost-versus-estimate picture, as important as it is, is but one of the many examples of actuals versus estimates in the world of the project. Each of these invites the interest of the project watchers from the company-level down to the task-level, broken down by department, by month, by subcontractor, a customer version, a supplier version and so on. To do all this you need a multi-dimensional system, created and supported for your unique corporate way of life. The system needs to offer value for money and be developed by a company specialising in project monitoring software. The advantage of buying in bespoke project monitoring software is that it relieves you of the task of creating your own project bureaucracy, including the need to keep an eye on the ever-changing details of the planning system you currently use, or the one you had thought of changing to. A caveat, a computer system is a Pandora's Box dressed up as a Trojan Horse. Pay someone else to keep the Augean Stables clean.

A computer system is a Pandora's Box dressed up as a Trojan Horse

Reports to the client: At project planning time you must agree with
the client as to what standard reports he requires and when. Then
make sure these reports are accurate and promulgated in a timely
manner. Of course, he will ask questions from time to time that no
one could have foreseen, requiring almost spontaneous action by
your Delphi operator.

Structuring the Reports

You have a variety of ways of accessing reports. Traditionally the
software would be housed in your own computer, cheek by jowl with the
Plan. But computer evolution makes it ever more fluent to access reports
via the Internet, though that is a detail that can change at any time. You, as
a user, may not be aware of it – and you shouldn't have to. Furthermore,
reports can be automated or ad-hoc. The decision is yours.

Below the global reports is a hierarchy of individual reports, including:-

What am I supposed to be doing? A bar chart showing each
person's planned hours during the ensuing period.

My Timesheet Actuals: Detailing individual hours that have been spent during a previous period.

Actuals versus Baseline: How is the project performing? Actuals versus Baseline for the various elements of the Project will give a clear view of how it is progressing and will flag up problem areas.

Resource requirements: Think of resource requirements as potholes in the road. Although they have all been filled in, as part of the initiation process, project life can nevertheless be prone to rough riding. A key problem is the incidence of people still engaged on other projects. This report shows the resource/availability situation, current and the immediate future, giving the project manager's resource tsar his daily charge sheet.

Make Reports Easy to Read and Absorb

Most of the information contained in the plethora of reports described consists of what we have done up to; at best, last night, vital but historical.

Remember, your enemy is reality

The choice of detail is wider than you'll ever need; from today's project software suppliers you can have whatever you like, whatever you (ie your people) think they need to do the job. But more immediate than anything is the "what-to-do-right-now" report: reality changes plans. And, of course, you have a change management process – and a practical way of incorporating changes. Remember, your enemy is reality. You must at all times bring reality and aspiration as close together as possible. The way to do this is to keep your focus on the thin red line of criticality; ensure that a report collating all the red lines in last night's version of the plan is on your screen when you come in the following morning, with hard copies for those who need them.

This Criticality Report must be simple, easy to read, sparse (unlike today's typical busy computer screen) and be prioritised in a way that suits your needs. However, if you can't make up your mind in what order to have things: have the task of shortest duration displayed at the top, and the longest at the bottom – a crude but defensible rule.

The next chapter ...

... is a short one but contains the discussion on the fundamental project manager's tool, PERT. And the fundamental problems, Elephant and Babel. Oratory.

Chapter 12: PERTry Not Poetry

Pert as a schoolgirl well can be

Gilbert and Sullivan

PERT in more detail

We introduced the idea of PERT in chapter 3, the basic numerical method of analysing a network. We shall now discuss it in more detail. It is an easy enough numerical technology, and should be of interest to everybody of the project persuasion: project owner, project manager, planner, individual workers and possibly the Chief Accountant, etc. But don't hold your breath. People get scared by detail.

As you begin to add the detail to the Project Plan, you begin to discover that it is an onion with a PERT chart at the centre. The layers of the onion are many and varied and there seems to be no limit to what they may consist of, depending on the needs of the project or the purposes to which the plan may be put. But whatever we do, it is unthinkable that the plan is not based ultimately on the tasks to be carried out, constrained only by logic, people, equipment, space, time, the ingenuity of the project manager, the patience of the customer, gravity, sunspots – and money.

Unfortunately, the PERT chart is often forgotten after the project has started. For those people working on the outer layers of the onion it may be largely invisible. Indeed, there is a strange inverse phenomenon to which I shall return later: the essential difference between a PERT chart and an elephant is that the larger the PERT chart the less likely you are to see it.

But the PERT chart is a simple enough concept. So what's the problem? Well there are at least two, and they are often passed over all too swiftly in the textbooks and on courses. Be warned, the problems are enough to defeat the planner, enrage the project manager and sabotage the project. They are the Elephant problem and the Babel problem.

The larger the PERT chart the less likely you are to see it

The Elephant Problem

Since their invention in the late 1940s computers have grown from a single K of memory to umpteen zillion nebubytes, following the well-known Decachip Law that the capacity of a computer at any point in time is equal to the total capacity of the world's computers a decade earlier. Nevertheless, throughout my project life I have always managed to accommodate myself within the confines of the computer memory supplied, which was just 1K when I started. In my experience, most people make do with what they can get from the industry.

My problem has always been access to that memory, and in this respect, things are getting worse, not better, as technology developers seem to promise. Hardware development these days is almost totally taken up with memory and speed to the detriment of accessibility. Punched cards disappeared in my youth and have been replaced with a screen only about ten times their size and at the same time memory has increased by some immeasurable power. Peering into today's vast computer by means of the palæoscreen is like examining an elephant with a microscope. For typing letters this is not a problem: we can still see most of an A4 sheet on the screen at any one time, and scrolling is quick. But project plans are not easily encompassed on A4 sheets let alone computer screens. In traditional guise, you can only accommodate some ten or so tasks of a PERT chart on an ordinary screen, and you can only double this if you use logic bar charts, as we discussed in Chapter 4, and that's it. Adding more tasks as we think of them is easy enough, but connecting them with constraint lines, at the same time as making them visible, gets more difficult as the number of tasks increases – to say nothing of the problem of removing unwanted tasks and their associated constraints and often having to patch in new constraints. This is the source of much error. A PERT or bar chart is a pictorial thing and should be dealt with pictorially. We want to be able to click on a predecessor and drag our constraint lines to the successor, however far away it is in the plan. If we have to key in task numbers via the keyboard much of the power of the screen is lost and a new source of error introduced. And if we have to convert geometry to algebra, solely because of the miniscule screen, we lose fluency.

The fundamental dilemma

As the size of the PERT chart increases to the point of becoming utterly unwieldy, and your wall ceases to be big enough to hold it, so we are faced with an unfortunate dilemma: the more we need to see the chart the less likely we are to do so.

Creating a project plan and using it as a management tool is not a sitting down job. It is a standing up and walking around job. To overcome the Elephant problem in a project planning system a disproportionate amount of system design and coding goes into the art of quickly refocusing the microscope, and reducing the amount of time spent switching back and forth between different views of the elephant rather than coping with the animal itself.

> **The (highly visible) tail would be seen as wagging the (unfortunately invisible) dog**

Instead of the conventional screen sitting on our desk, what we need is a flat screen fixed to the wall, some six conventional screens wide, say, by four high, displaying twenty or thirty times as much information at a time: big enough to trace a constraint line across a large swathe of plan without scrolling and thereby losing the thread. Use the keyboard for initiating the data, task names, durations, etc., but be able to use your fingertips to manipulate it. You can then plan in decent subproject-size chunks, linking the subprojects at a higher level with the same visibility.

If what I say is true, why haven't we been issued with such screens? I have been nagging the planning system suppliers for years, and I am not alone. The technology is there, but so is the inertia. This is because most of our systems sit inside PCs, and because they are relatively cheap they are perceived as minor budget items. However, attaching relatively expensive display devices to them would be regarded as a disproportionate cost outlay; the (highly visible) tail would be seen as wagging the (unfortunately invisible) dog. What is not directly apparent is that the value of the data constituting a project plan is usually many orders of magnitude greater than the cost of either the PC or the planning system. It's like the value of the company versus a day's pay of the managing director.

So join the crusade and ask for wide screen technology to acquire a better balance between magnitude and manipulation.

The Babel Problem

The Elephant problem is the easy part. The hard part is producing a PERT chart in the first place – the Babel problem. It is the process of hooking together contributions from a wide variety of disciplines, each with its own arcane language, under the leadership of a project manager who probably isn't a specialist in more than one field, and may have little more than a superficial understanding of the others.

There is much more to this problem than you ever see in the books or journals. The reason for this is not that there is any conspiracy of silence, but rather that the PERT chartists of the world are so immersed in their labours that they don't have the time to tell you how they do it. This is very remiss of us and we must make amends. We all have our methods of dealing with it and I discuss mine in Chapter 13.

Beware Oratory

But why the title of this chapter? It is more than a gimmick. It concisely explains why we make plans at all. One of the weaknesses in the genetic makeup of *Homo sapiens* is that we have very little mental defence against oratory; the world is full of impressive speakers. They have deep voices and are six feet tall, even when they're sitting down at the meeting table. If you're not careful they will carry the day. We are all of us gullible, and most bad ideas sound like good ones to start with, when the oratory is persuasive.

The world is full of impressive speakers

The only defence you have against company-destroying oratory is an honest model of what the man is saying. And the best form of modelling or simulation is of course the detailed PERT chart. It won't be complete; it isn't reality. But it's far better than hot air (of which there is too much already on this planet). Another way of saying all this is that ...

...PERT is a defence mechanism for small people with squeaky voices. It enables the meek to inherit the earth, and is the best hope you have of a successful project

---

The next chapter ...

... is about creating the plan with all involved – turmoil in the Tower of Babel. Popularity. The windowless room. The phases. The cost.

Chapter 13: Turmoil in the Tower

And from this chasm, with ceaseless turmoil seething

Coleridge

More on the Babel Problem

This chapter discusses a lot of detail, which is primarily the responsibility of the project manager. Although the minutiae may cause profound eye-glazing on the part of the project owner, it is beneficial if he is present on at least Day Zero of this process. It has the valuable effect of revealing both the complication of the project and the incisive managerial instincts of the project manager, thereby forever cementing their vital relationship. In this chapter the "you" means either of project owner or manager, where e'er the cap fits.

In Chapter 12, PERTry Not Poetry, I discussed two of the problems facing the project planner or manager, the "Elephant Problem" and the "Babel Problem" – getting people to understand the scope of the PERT chart and coping with it in today's world of computing power. I now want to discuss the problem of producing a PERT chart in the first place – the Babel Problem. Doing so can also be regarded as a bridge between the Project Initiation phase and the project proper.

In the traditional organisation all is calm

In the traditional organisation, all is calm. Each department has its well-defined job to do and it does it with a minimum of clamour. Company procedures, in true Darwinian fashion, have been evolved from the time the company was founded. Standards have been set according to regulations of one sort and another, and entered into the company Standards Manual. People have found their rightful place in the scheme of things – hopefully kept at a level where they can do most good or least harm, i.e. as close to the bottom as possible. And each speaks to the other in a language appropriate to the departmental function – even though individuals hail from distant parts of the globe: a Mongolian and an English electrical engineer have a closer language than two Englishmen, one an advertising executive and the other a circus clown.

Departments are very comfortable structures to work in. This is not so for projects. A typical project will be populated by people from all walks of working life: all the shades of engineering, manufacturing, legal, finance, art, politics, advertising and so on. The Tower of Babel has nothing on the modern project for a multiplicity of languages. This is the problem this chapter will address. It crops up every day and not least at the birth of a project when the first PERT chart is created.

No single person speaks all the languages spoken in the course of a project – and that includes the project manager as much as anybody else. There is no particular discipline, which is more appropriate to project management than any other. Project management expertise is derived exclusively from the act of managing projects. Since a project manager is probably fluent in at most one of the discipline languages of his team, he could just as easily be a lawyer or computer programmer as a design engineer or financial adviser. Whoever he is, his first task is to create the PERT chart that will help determine how long the project might take to carry out, how much it might cost, whether the resources are available, whether the idea is viable, and so on. In doing this he has to talk intelligibly in a multiplicity of tongues, often with a team of people who have never met before; suspicion and incomprehensibility rule the day – at least on Day Zero. So what do you do?

Learn From One's Mistakes

I'll start out by telling you what not to do. I learned this the first time I tried to run a project. It was so long ago we had no project computer system.

PERT existed more as an idea deeply hidden in the textbooks than as a usable management tool.

**If we're fortunate enough we all find ourselves
at some time or another on the road to Damascus**

The people involved had their offices spread over a wide geographical area, and didn't talk much to one another. The person with the project idea was an incorrigible introvert, and I only had a vague notion of what it was all about. However, enough luck was on my side to get started. One of the secretaries, by happy chance, knew the names of enough bright guys in the various design departments to give me someone to talk to. (As I said in the Introduction, one of the tragedies brought about by the personal computer has been the abolition of the secretarial function. I hope I am not alone in recognising its erstwhile value as the core of the corporate knowledge system.) To find out more I naively sent out a memo to my nascent project team telling them, vaguely of course, what the ultimate idea was, and asking them for their portion of the PERT chart by Friday afternoon. I would spend Saturday morning piecing together the jigsaw so that we could get cracking the following week. Or so I naively wrote. If we are fortunate, we all find ourselves at some time or another on the road to Damascus and never look back.

Which brings us on to **Old Norman's Law of Learning**: The key to success in learning things in this life is to be fortunate enough to surround yourself with patient, friendly people who are willing to straighten you out.

**Surround yourself with patient, friendly
people willing to straighten you out**

Old Norman's Law of Learning has several corollaries, two of which
are as follows:

Management is a popularity contest

To be a successful manager you need to surround yourself with people
who want to straighten you out, who take a pernicious delight in doing so,
who want the world to know that you're an idiot – in the nicest possible
way of course. The ultimate problem of the manager is knowing what
the questions are. But you can't do this in a vacuum. There are too many
questions; you're not clever enough and you don't have the time. You need
friends – or even better, vociferous enemies – who will tell you what the
answers are even without your asking the questions.

Failure is the secret of success

If you get it right first time you'll never know why. You won't have learnt
anything. If you get it wrong and fix it you'll understand it. Even Sir Isaac
Newton made mistakes. Fortunately for Newton he had a vociferous enemy
in Robert Hooke. Hooke exposed Newton's errors with consummate glee
to the fellows of the Royal Society, forcing Newton to redo the necessary

mathematics to get it right. (NB. Hooke himself, though a brilliant scientist in his own right, was not a consummate mathematician.)

Meanwhile, back at the ranch, I wish I had kept the bits of paper I got back from my historical memo. No one today would believe it. Each of the addressees replied, each according to his own culture, encapsulated in his technical language and illustrated by diagrams, no two of which bore any relation to one another. Crick and Watson had an easier time getting the base molecular structures to fit. It was far from your fully interlocking 5000-piece jigsaw! No one had anticipated the contribution of the others. Each had acted as if on a planet of their own. I learnt nothing of the details of the project, but I did learn that PERT was in its infancy and that a little dialogue would be necessary. But what I did in those pre-computer days (and I'm sure I wasn't alone) is still valid today, and should still be used by any project manager who wants to get off to a good start. So it's more than of solely historical interest. The computer has only made it more important because it encourages detail and thereby acts as a catalyst. This is what you do:

The Windowless Room

You find a windowless room with two long walls. You remove the pictures of the Founder and the Chairman of the Board, and you cover both walls with white paper, from ceiling to floor. You find a stepladder on wheels, a pencil, some felt pens of various colours, a camera and an energetic secretary/personal assistant. Book the room for two or three days, lay on some bread and water and invite your nucleus team (the discipline leaders, responsible for the detailed work of their subordinates) to a siege. Only experience can give you any understanding of the ensuing battle. All I can do is give you some indication. It's like talking to the blind about colour.

The development of the Project Plan consists of a series of phases as follows:-

The Suspicion Phase

When the team is first assembled its members probably haven't met one another before. Moreover, they may have very little knowledge of one another's disciplines: the electrical chap couldn't put a shelf up to save his life, and the piping chap couldn't change a light bulb. Yet they have the collective task of creating some single entity, each relying on the others to provide their components.

The Suspicion Phase

The first hour or two are fraught with suspicion. Each member, naturally, regards his own job as the only important one. The others are there in a support capacity and don't really understand what it's all about. Anyway, they can't be much good otherwise they'd be too busy to be put on a crummy project like this one! No one moves. Each eyes the others, and you have a very uncomfortable time getting some energy and direction into the situation. A most inauspicious start, though an inevitable one.

The Confusion Phase

But be of good cheer. The secret is to know that you can start absolutely anywhere. The important thing is to make a start. That's what project management is all about. So you point to any member of the team and ask him what his first task will be. After a couple of false starts, the selected member will identify his first task. Call it Task 1. The assistant will draw a box in the middle of paper-covered Wall 1, standing on the third rung of the step ladder, in pencil. In the box he will write a description of the task, perhaps a clue as to what resources might be needed, but no attempt at a time estimate. That would be far too premature.

At this step you have already done your job. You have made the most important contribution of the day and can now sit back in your chair, allow your eyes to acquire a patina of glaze and let PERT take over. From then on PERT speaks through the medium of the project manager, which explains why project managers always appear to be in a trance.

> **Better the confusion of the Big Bang
> than no creation at all!**

PERT asks the assembled company what preceding task must be finished before the person in the spotlight can start on his chosen first one. At first, there is silence while people try to understand what was said. There is a trickle, then a stream, then a cascade of rival candidates for the task immediately preceding Task 1. The poor Project Secretary scoots up and down the stepladder, drawing, writing and erasing, as you conduct your orchestra as if in a symphony by Mahler.

You know that you need only three preceding tasks, so you select the most likely from the many suggestions when you've had enough of the shouting. We will return to the others later.

Then the discussion moves on to what tasks will be able to follow Task 1. The contributor of Task 1 may not care, but some of the others will have ideas. Move the stepladder and write them down. You now have a smidgen of a network.

After that little bit of serial activity, you broaden the remit to include possible parallel tasks that can take place at the same time as Task 1 and its neighbours. This creates another burst of confusion. But out of it will crystallise a set of fairly independent subsets of the network, and these will begin inevitably to reflect the physical nature of the product structure beginning to emerge from the primeval chaos. In aircraft manufacture, for example, the body and wing assemblies take place in parallel until the wing-body join task, and this will show in the PERT chart as two networks coming together towards the right hand side of the sheet, much akin to the pictures of constellations that today's telescopes are taking – though on a more modest scale.

This phase will create more heat than light, but by the end of it an exhausted Project Secretary will have produced a spaghetti-like picture of about twenty tasks, the most lyrical representation of confusion you will have ever seen. But better the confusion of the Big Bang than no creation at all!

Thus endeth the first day, a veritable Balthazar's feast. Before starting the second day redraw the spaghetti on Wall 1 in a more lasagne-like way on Wall 2, minimising the routes taken by the constraints, making it easier to handle Day 2's continued development of the network. Do this with the felt pen, colour-coding the various disciplines, and take a picture for the record.

The Educational Phase

By Day 2 the team members will have got to know one another a little bit, especially if you have arranged a little nocturnal team-building in the meantime. Confidence and understanding will have begun to replace the initial suspicion. Although the picture on the wall will not be easy to understand at a glance, because it has been built up in detail by painstaking detail by the team, the team will understand its scope.

As the diagram develops, more and more descriptive information will be written on it. As this happens, try to make this as structured as possible. In addition to colour-coding the tasks, number them in some semblance of order; you will convert these into task IDs and Names later. Use short versions of the task descriptions on the picture itself, at the same time get the discipline leaders to write the full versions on their note pads. Where the constraint lines are too long, cut them short and use Greek letters for identifying connections. Remember to make frequent use of the camera.

The wall becomes our common enemy

Day 2 will produce three times as many tasks as Day 1, bringing the total up to around eighty, enough for the wall version of any PERT chart. During the day, mutual understanding and agreement will accelerate, and from it will already emerge an understanding of the project at a level of detail unprecedented by any previous discussion.

Hitherto hidden problems will have emerged: research items where the current technology isn't up to scratch; doubts perhaps about the market; estimates of budget which are much higher than initially thought. However, remember what we said about experimental tasks. Don't mix them up with well-understood tasks. They can be deadly saboteurs.

Note that so far we have not made any use of the computer. All we are doing is readying ourselves for it. This is a very interesting parenthetical point. During the build-up of the network, the paper on the wall takes on a life of its own and begins to dominate the proceedings. The wall makes discoveries. It tells us things. It becomes our common enemy and unites us in attacking it. The eventual use of the computer acts as the catalyst to optimising the way things are done. During this phase, it appears through its surrogate, the wall.

The Subnet Phase

If Day 2 finishes with a PERT chart of eighty, or at most a hundred tasks and their accompanying web of constraints, you have done very well, though you might find it takes closer to a week to get that far.

On Wall 1, select those tasks that contain the most work and expand them, one by one, into individual networks in their own right. Out of a hundred tasks, you might find ten that need this extra layer of detail. We call these subnets. And you might even find that an occasional task in a subnet that needs a further level of detail.

When should this process finish? A rule of thumb is that a PERT chart should contain fewer than a hundred tasks (before counting the subnets). A good criterion to apply is that the effort required in each of the lowest level tasks should be broadly similar. But we haven't talked about effort yet, so we are jumping the gun a bit here.

The Computer Phase

When Wall 2 has been covered with a top-level network and Wall 1 with subnet details, your team will be exhausted, the stepladder bent hopelessly out of shape and your Project Secretary has resigned for the fifth time in a week. It is time to stop. You've gone far enough. You have reached the stage where the volume of information has forced you onto the computer.

If you have done a decent job of identifying the tasks and constraints with colours and numbers, and photographed them systematically, it will be a relatively easy job to enter the components of the PERT chart into the computer. Although you may have difficulty acquiring a large screen to attach to your PC for input purposes, there is a wide selection of large printers available, making it possible to print out acres of resulting PERT. So, it is back to the wall to use the computer printouts of PERT charts for continued discussions with project members, probably extending the discussion to a wider range of people who are closer to the detail.

The Time Estimate Phase

At this point you have created the topology of the PERT chart, but you can't analyse or schedule it, i.e. you can't turn it into a plan, because it lacks the time estimates associated with each activity. While the nucleus team, the discipline leaders, have specified the nature of the tasks and their constraints, they are unlikely to be the best people for giving you the time estimates. *Old Norman's Law of Time Estimates* states that accuracy of estimates varies inversely with distance from the detail.

Workers love to catch the bosses out

The best people to estimate the effort required to do anything are those most closely connected with it. Let them name their own poison. You'd think this was blindingly obvious, but many a project has been sabotaged by high level estimating infused with corporate politics and optimism. (The world's worst example of this is the British National Health System launched in 2002 where it seems that somebody mistook a billion for a million with adenoids.) So roll up your PERT chart, jump on your bike and visit the front line resources. Have them write down their estimates of the man-hours required in the boxes provided, together with their availability, and sign them up; your contract with your people. In doing so you will inevitably be received with hollow laughter as errors and omissions are rectified in the top level version of the PERT chart. Workers love to catch bosses out – a corporate anthropological feature that helps get things right. And it could be that one or other of these renders the whole enterprise impossible – if so the sooner we know about it the better.

And in attaching the time estimates please remember that optimism is both a survival factor and a source of sabotage. The species *Homo sapiens* has survived mainly because of its optimism.

**The species *Homo sapiens* has survived
mainly because of its optimism**

Despite history being the history of disaster, we get up each morning and go whistling down the road as though nothing could go wrong. But if there's a project at the end of the road it will surely be infected. Your best protection against optimistic contagion is your PERT chart. You have invested substantial effort in producing it in the first place, keep it by your side at all times and produce it whenever anybody sneezes.

But How Much Will it All Cost?

One of the beauties of the PERT chart is that the project budget is a more or less effortless by-product. Oh that company finance departments and Cabinet Ministers would understand this! How often do they put the budget cart before the PERT horse! All that remains is to apply average hourly rates to the man-hour estimates and complete the resource assignments task by task: materials, equipment, workplaces, etc. In seconds, you have the total project budget and whatever S-curves you might need for funding purposes, your input to the plans of your finance department. All computer planning systems do this as standard practice.

And There You Have it!

By now you have all you could possibly need to embark on your project, your PERT chart and all it stands for – including not least the catalytic value of welding you and your team together. In undertaking the often-traumatic process of producing it, you have learned a lot, certainly enough to hit the deck running on Day Zero of the project. That alone will have been well worth the effort.

The next chapter ...

...is about using the project planning system beyond the project itself. Budgets. The documentation spine. Italian databases. The cold shower. Internal contracts. Approval document. Winning contracts. External contracts. The corporate brake. Management milestones. A learning device. Life-long learning. Corporate learning.

Chapter 14: A Postscript – Getting the Most From Your Project Plans

> *When he wrote a letter he would put that which was most material in the postscript*
>
> Francis Bacon

A Multiplicity of Uses

The primary reason for the existence of the project planning system is, as the name says, it helps plan projects. However, the system has a multiplicity of uses beyond the plan itself, both within the project community and in the broader organisation. This chapter is primarily aimed at the project manager and planner but can also be of value to people in non-project departments, not least in the finance department. That this is not fully appreciated is probably due to the words project and planning in the names and the sad fact that project and staff people rarely talk to one another; perhaps it is because they don't have much in common to talk about. Each side lays hidden unobtrusively behind the universal corporate culture screen. But we project folk can come to the rescue of those in the staff. To make contact all you need do is copy the last section of this chapter, Spreading the Word – The Plan as Anyone's Budget Document, and hand it to your Finance Department. It might get them to borrow the whole book and take heed of other ideas that apply also to the non-project world – though don't stand around waiting on one leg for this to happen.

The Plan as a Cold Shower

Experience shows that trying to plan a project can prove that for reasons other than money the project isn't possible. The budget procedure, unaccompanied by a viable plan, does not force you to think of the details of actually spending the money. Whether or not you are involved in a project, the budget plan enables you to make discoveries or to stumble on weaknesses that had not been obvious to date, and in doing so it enables you to make amendments well before they hit you during the life of the project itself. This will give you a sporting chance of being able to do something about it. But as the day approaches on which you have to give reasons for your justification and think about the details of implementing your grand idea, you may find you have no time or resources with which to do it. In November you thought you would be able to install that machine in May because you had no other plans at all for May. But the winds of March and the showers of April have brought with them trials and tribulations you might well have foreseen had you taken the trouble. It is better to plan it all in detail, at budget time, and discover that the resources aren't going to be there to do the work or manage it, and admit disappointment (though not defeat). The alternative is to wait until the something or other happens, which forces activity to stop, gather dust and quieten down the jovial remarks out in the corridors. A good case should be made for the value of a discarded plan being of greater value than that of an adopted one. To spend a small amount of money to prevent a large amount of waste is not a bad thing.

> # Budgets don't provoke much thought!

Making the logic visible and showing inevitable conflicts for resources is a revealing and often sobering experience. Budgets don't provoke much thought! Plans do. If it can't be planned it can't be done. So it could be that you don't have a project on your hands after all. If so, the sooner you swallow any residual pride the better. All it cost you was a few hours of time at the keyboard in the isolation of your cubicle. No materials, no invoices, no loss of prestige, no wasted time. Make sure the message gets up the line and become a corporate hero. You don't often get the chance.

The Plan as the Spine Document

Whether you are working within the confines of a project, or not, always act as though you are. People the world over are communicating, and writing like never before, even those to whom writing had hitherto not come naturally – all catalysed by the now ubiquitous internet. Who reads it all is another matter; it is one of the imponderables of modern life. But sadly this cornucopia of words has not yet stretched to the documentation of projects. Like most people, project people will gladly tell you their life stories en route from London to Sidney, but getting them to explain what they're doing on the project, what percent is finished and so on, is not easy. Solving this problem requires a document structure – as before, catalysed by the project plan sitting on the computer, and perhaps by a quality control system. If you make it easy for them there's no escape. (You could even think of tying it into the payroll system, but I wouldn't recommend it.)

If the author of a document cannot find a corresponding ID

This section is about documentation in all its glory, project and non-project. The key to success is to use the Plan as the Spine Document or Document Register, a backbone linking all the documentation of the project. The idea is that each task shall contain a reference to all the documents pertaining to it, of whatever nature, and all documents, be they memos, drawings, purchase orders, contractual items, invoices or lawyers' letters, shall bear the IDs of the relevant tasks involved: a many-to-one relationship in both directions. If the author of a document cannot find a corresponding ID, then something is missing from the plan, and needs to be interpolated. Here's where you really need the tail to wag the dog so that there is then no doubt which of the many orders, deliveries, meetings, printing machines or brick walls the man is talking about. Additionally, if the plan is embellished within an Information Container for memo numbers, purchase order numbers and amounts, and reminders to Charlie not to forget the glue, little will be forgotten.

Here's where you really want
the tail to wag the dog

Many of the documents will probably originate outside the project, in which case suppliers etc shall be trained to include the appropriate IDs at the top left hand corner. And if they can't find one they inform the Documents Received group (or person) in the project office who identifies the suspects and, in pure self-defence, enters the ID themselves.

You could even teach them a little doggerel:

If you remember the ID we'll
pay you on Friday

However, the source of most of the project documentation is the plan itself, both at the planning stage and during execution, and the best place to initiate the writing is right there in the task data. Most planning systems provide for this by including a Task Information Field. Returning to our simple bar chart illustrated in Chapter 4:

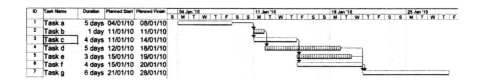

Logic Bar Chart

If we double-click on, say, ID 3, Task c, we get a whole host of information about the task created by the analysis and the schedule:

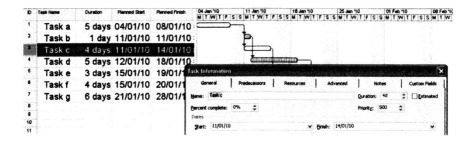

Logic Bar Chart: Task c Basic Information

We can now click on Notes, a blank sheet on which we can write anything of importance. Moreover we can do it on the fly before we forget about it, and it can be either diary entries or instructions for action:-

Task Information						✕
General	Predecessors	Resources	Advanced	Notes	Custom Fields	

Name: Task c   Duration: 4d   ☐ Estimated

Notes:

| A | ▤ | ▤ | ▤ | ☰ | 🖼 |

1) 9/01/10 Concrete mixer may get delayed. Charlie please expedite.

2) 10/01/10 Still hasn't arrived. Task may start late.

3) 11/01/10 Delivered middle of the night.

4) 13/01/10 Only half the cement delivered. Charlie!

5) 15/01/10 Remaining cement delivered. Went into overtime. Task completed today.

Logic Bar Chart: Task c Notes

At each report time, the concatenation of all the task notes then constitutes the bottom level of each report, leaving it to the Project Secretary to write a compacted version readable by the Important People. Making it easy to harvest the raw writing in this way solves the perennial problem of exacting sentences as a task in itself by people unfamiliar with the art of writing.

This takes care of the documentation created by the plan. In addition to this, however, we have the documents emanating from outside the plan. How do we do this? In Chapter 4 we started to create the fields contained in each task in the Project Plan, reaching the point at which we could perform an analysis. However, we also said that the task data set contained a large number of other fields, in theory perhaps a hundred per task. Included here can be pointers to the types of external documents, each containing a number system: the Drawing Register Pointer, (DRP), the Accounts Receivable Pointer, (ARP), the Accounts Payable Pointer (APP) and so on:-

TASK NAME								
DU	ID	ES	EF	LS	LF	ERP	ARP	APP

A pointer consists of a table containing references to each document within its purview or scope, making it easy to locate. This sounds like bureaucracy, and it is bureaucracy, but it is good bureaucracy. It has to be experienced to be believed. Tie all your documentation to the plan via the ID numbers. It is so simple, so valuable, and sadly so ignored. And if you can't find the ID then someone has omitted the task from the plan, and a bit of replanning will have to take place (as we said above and will say again below).

The Plan as a Defence Mechanism Against Italian Databases

The purpose of the Spine Document is to identify the documents. An associated supplementary to the Spine Document is a mechanism to actually handle the documents, to know at all times where they are and what's supposed to be happening to them. The most interesting (pre-computer) database I have ever encountered was that of the Italian Automobile Club, the ACI. It was contained in a vast room, consisting of an elliptical counter measuring some twenty metres by ten, manned by a single occupant, the Lord of the Files (il Signore degli Archivi). The database itself comprised a veritable mountain of documents, of every function, colour, shape, layout, etc. and state of preservation, pertaining to motorcars. His lordship made little effort to welcome the intruder, but was amazingly adept at locating your sought-after document. This was job security Italian style and when they came to retire him they inherited a data-retrieval problem beyond the trowel of any archaeologist. Don't do this. Instead, use the plan as the hub of a Document Management System (DMS) – again supplied by your systems company.

The Lord of the Files

The Plan as an Internal Contract

One of the most frequent complaints you get from the internal (company) project members (as opposed to the outside contractors) is that, because they find themselves oscillating between one project and another, they don't really feel sufficiently dedicated to any: no single item is their top priority; it's not part of their department; they only work here. It's not difficult running an enthusiastic planning meeting before the project has been blessed with budget. That's fun and a welcome temporary relief from the normal drudgery of the working day; the prospect of the friction-free and gravity-free world out there in the dim and distant future, doing something exciting. They are with you all the way – until it starts! Somehow, you must get the team and their department managers to commit to the project. If this is not done at the start when all is light, it certainly won't be easy when reality starts hitting the fan, the going gets tough and the lights go out. Having convinced the stakeholders that your plan is as realistic as it can possibly be made, the last thing you do before starting to turn theory into reality is to have them all sign it.

We're with you all the way – until it starts

Everyone involved must sign the Commitment Document: the production department heads (this will get you all the internal people you have asked for, when you need them); the legal department (getting you all the contract people you need, when you need them); the head of finance (you now have the authority to buy the equipment and material resources you have asked for without any delay); your immediate boss (he becomes fully aware of the assumptions you have made, the risks you are taking, the commitments the production departments have made, and is backing you all the way); and the general manager (giving you the backing of the entire company).

This document is known as the ha-bloody-ha list

The front cover needs to contain as many signatures as it takes to be allowed to climb Mount Everest! This document is known as the ha-bloody-ha list. But it's what you will need should it be necessary to wade the corporate Rubicon a year or two from now.

The Plan as the Approval Document

You now take your company-backed plan to the project owner for him to give you corporate approval to run the project; delegating to you the authority and assigning to you the responsibility. All good textbook stuff.

It's all systems go, and the only reason now for delaying or cancelling the project is either that at the eleventh hour it is deemed to have become too expensive or that other contenders for investment money have wangled a higher priority. Unless neither of these disasters happens, the plan is now an internal contract, tantamount to a legal document, and should include the documents signed by the outside contractors.

The Plan as an Aid in Getting the Contract

In a competitive situation, including your plan in the contract documents is a very powerful ploy. I realised this when the German head of one of my subsidiaries suffered an attack of apoplexy on discovering what I'd done. But I have seen this mean the difference between success and failure. This is particularly true if your price might give the impression to the prospective customer that you're expensive. Put their boardroom table to good use for once. Roll out your printed PERT chart on it and invite them to conduct a minute investigation. Let the plan be the principal discussion document. Invite them to use it to ask the questions. Challenge them to remove any task or reduce any time estimate. Challenge them to compare your plan with those of the competition (if they have one). And above all, include the tasks that they are responsible for and make them understand that they are part of the project; bring them into your team. If you play with open cards you will strengthen your case beyond recognition.

The Plan as Part of the Customer Contract

In the same vein as the above, in the case of a contract for an outside customer, the approved plan should be included, perhaps as an appendix, and it can be very useful during the actual process of obtaining the contract in the first place. It helps to convince the customer that we know what we are doing, that we can deliver the goods by the contracted time. Moreover, a project often requires that a customer carries out certain tasks himself to dovetail in with your own. He may have to prepare facilities in time for your installation, or have his operators show up for training. If the plan is part of the contract, all inter-company finger-pointing will be averted. Moreover, the customer's attendance should be mandatory at project review meetings where their tasks are up for discussion. The contract should clearly specify that all departures from the plan caused by the customer, including the specification of the product or the work done to achieve it, shall be paid for by the customer. Likewise, all departures caused by the supplier shall be paid for by the supplier. If the plan is right there in the contract as the neutral evidence of what was agreed to, there should be little problem in achieving this. Indeed, in principle, any change caused by the customer becomes a new contract. In practice, of course, the evolving contract consists of the original version plus a series of Variation Orders. (See Chapter 6 for a discussion of Variation Orders.)

The Plan as a Corporate Braking System

Never spend good money chasing bad. Even though you did everything you could to simulate the project in your plan – the engineer said it would work; the salesman said it would sell; the maintenance man said it wouldn't need fixing; the accountant said the sums all added up – the ultimate test is reality, and halfway through the life of the project you made a terrible discovery. It is not viable!

> **There have only been about five successful generals in the history of warfare**

If someone on high isn't made aware of it in time nothing will stop the momentum – which will only increase because of the additional work needed to fix the unfixable. It is of course the project manager's job to keep the project owner appraised of progress or lack thereof, but no one likes to be the bearer of bad tidings – at least if their possibility hasn't been anticipated. There have only been about five successful generals in the history of warfare. The Duke of Wellington (again) was one of these precisely because he foresaw the possibility of defeat and therefore always made contingency plans: if his troops had to retreat it was always to well-prepared defences, built by his reserves and held in readiness. If the defences weren't needed it meant he had won the battle, and his reserves had had an opportunity of practicing building fortifications. The Duke was one of the all time great project managers, from whom we have much to learn. In the modern project world contingency plans are simply fall-back positions to be taken at the management milestones.

> **Only in the classroom is it wrong to be wrong**

Every good planner plans in phases, each phase terminating in a management review, one possible consequence of which should be the termination of the project itself (unless the project is building a bridge). Remember, the general manager has signed page one agreeing beforehand to allow this to happen. No amount of discussion, artist's impressions, plans, speeches or dreams can supplant the experience gained in trying to convert those dreams into reality. It is not a hanging offence to discover during the early phases something otherwise unpredictable that renders the later phases impracticable or too expensive. Only in the classroom is it wrong to be wrong – according to the teachers.

If the initial plan clearly depicts the existence of the management milestones and the reasons for them, then the project go-ahead must by implication allow and bless the possibility of so-called failure. If you prepare for possible failure and bring the project owner in on the preparations, then you should have no problem applying the corporate brakes that every project should contain. You cross your Rubicon with your army of signatories, the signed plan your shield and buckler.

The Plan as the Lord Mayor's Show

After the Lord Mayor's Show comes the man with the bucket and shovel. In our case, as the project moves along, if you discover any document that doesn't bear an ID, and no such task exists, then you know you've left something out; a new piece of PERT needs shovelling into the bucket.

> **Let reality guide your planning hand**

Fill the bucket and use its contents to add fertiliser to your plan where needed. Let reality guide your planning hand right through to the bitter end so that you finish with a complete picture of what happened. Someone might need that completed plan as the starting point of some subsequent project. That person could even be you.

Having Fun - The Plan as a Learning Device

The only way to succeed is to fail. The only way to get things right is to first get them wrong. If you get it right the first time, you will never know why. If you win a game of Master Mind with just one row, it will be pure luck. Only by making a long series of (non-fatal) mistakes can you learn in life.

> **The only way to succeed is to fail**

One of the key factors that separates *Homo sapiens* from butterflies, tigers and squids is retrospection, the ability to look back critically and learn from past events.

For much of human endeavour accuracy doesn't matter, and when we write our memoirs we indulge in permissible poetic recollection. But it does matter in the world of business. We have to be competitive and profitable, but unaided human memory isn't a reliable basis for either.

The ability to look back critically on past events

So everything you do must be in relation to some sort of expectation. In our case the expectation consists, of course, in the plan; PERTry not poetry. We compare the actuals with what we expected and we take the trouble to find out why the two didn't tally, where the variances were and why they occurred. And it's a big surprise every time!

During the life of the Project, we input data and use the computer to tell us what the consequences are, helping us explain them to others. Reality replaces hope and theory, and the plan is remade from time to time. The true course will deviate from the plan. It should be compared to the Baseline, the initial pristine version, before it becomes contaminated by reality. Dates will slide, costs will mount and the profit margin of the project will diminish.

There are two candidates for updating, of course, time and cost. Of these, time is unavoidable. If you don't reassess the remaining time needed to complete each task you soon blunt your management tool. Part of the value of doing anything is learning how to do it; DIY means life-long learning. The Remaining Duration of a task gets progressively more accurate compared to the initial estimate, right down to the final microsecond. As we replan the remainder of the project, the plan gets more accurate. It's just like landing an aircraft in a high cross-wind. The pilot has an enormous number of corrections to perform at a very high speed. It's only when you have finished doing something that you understand what you had to do. Hence **Old Norman's Law of Computer Programming:** the best time to write a computer program is immediately you've successfully used it. Thus the corollary **Old Norman's Law of Project Planning:** the best time to make a plan is when you've successfully completed the project.

DIY means life-long learning

On the other hand, you can survive without reporting costs into the system, the number of hours worked on each task, the materials consumed, etc. But if you ignore costs today you will continue to repeat the same mistakes tomorrow and the opportunity of profiting from corporate experience (see below) is lost.

Unfortunately, many companies, even though browbeaten into making a plan in the first place, don't see the necessity of collecting and reporting man-hours and dates, and they never therefore learn anything. It takes effort, which they regard as misspent resources, to keep their plans up to date. In the process they waste the most important long-term assets of the plan: they don't learn anything – and they don't have any fun! If you have never passed beyond the stage of making the plan you have never known the fun of learning from it. Entering actual values of time and money spent, comparing them with what you thought they would be is, believe it or not, an exhilarating experience. The learning you derive from it is what eventually separates the sheep from the goats in the field of project management.

The Plan as a Receptacle for Corporate Experience

One of the facts that you very quickly learn is that *Homo sapiens* is an incorrigible optimist. Optimism is a species survival factor. We only remember the good things, or we think that next time around things will automatically be better; they can't be this bad again! (The stock market will always rebound.) But last time's reality is a far better start to a new Project Plan than this time's theory. On the other hand last time's reality is only available if you have collected it systematically making available for next time. So, as I've said before, ad nauseam, collect and report everything that happens to the plan this time, and use this information as the starting point next time – with, of course, suitable modifications depending on circumstances. (Everyone should have a Lessons Learned Log.)

Spreading the Word – The Plan as Anyone's Budget Document

Finally, the plan as an all-pervading, non-project tool. The following is a golden opportunity for a manager, say, to make himself a hero throughout the company, not just in the project component.

Second only to the calendar-handling features of the planning system is its ability to handle budgets: not only project budgets, but any budget at all. To create a budget, you need to know what you're going to do, how long it's going to take, what equipment you are going to need: premises, machinery, materials, etc, and the unit costs of all these items. But you don't necessarily need to know when you're going to do it – unless it spans more than one financial period. The requirements of the standard corporate budget are essentially identical to the requirements of the project budget except for the need for logical constraints linking the tasks involved. The component parts of the budget activities may not necessarily be connected – but your project planning system does not force you to invent any. And it doesn't even force you to enter any dates: for budget purposes you can imagine that it all takes place at the same time. Indeed, you may not even know precisely when, during the year, the component tasks will take place. Thus everything that an organisation decides it wants to do may be regarded as quasi, logic-free projects. (Like the friction-free and gravity-free human mind.) So, in addition to your project concerns, as you read this try to think of non-project activities that could use the system. Spread project planning knowledge beyond the limits prescribed by project requirements; if you can get anyone to listen.

Back to the project for a moment. Project plans have been successfully made since the early Mesopotamians tamed the Delta, the Chinese built their wall and the Egyptians built the pyramids, all with very little help from the computer. As a consequence a lot of detail was ignored, not least the cost of it all. On the other hand not much money changed hands during the lives of projects in those days, so there was little need for detailed budgets.

> ## You can't fool a computer with vague ideas

Today, however, whether you are involved in a project or not, if you use a computer you are forced to understand the problem at a minute level of detail; at a level much more detailed than ever before. It is easy enough during the budget round in November to write a large number down on a piece of paper, accompanied by some creative writing and a diagram or two; your paragraph of justification for something to happen next May. But you can't fool a computer with vague ideas; a computer is a harder taskmaster than your managing director. You have to be precise and you have to be complete. Thus a computerised plan inevitably contains so much detail that a credible budget is an automatic by-product. If the tasks are anywhere near comprehensive, and the rates for the work accurate, it's all done for you.

Budgeting without a plan is worthless, while budgeting as a result of a plan is effortless. So the final step in the project acceptance procedure is to compare the initial, pre-plan financial estimates with data extracted from the plan. The latter will come as a tectonic shock at the head office if its inhabitants haven't been following events closely.

> **Budgeting without a plan is worthless, while budgeting as a result of a plan is effortless**

So, be warned, planned budgets always exceed the annual budget-round versions. Even if you aren't dealing with a project you can pretend to be doing so and make every budget a pseudo-project.

The annual budget-round figure is too small

Conclusion

The purpose of this chapter has been to broaden the mind and enlarge the scope of using a planning system more broadly within the project – and beyond the confines of the project. There is much more potential in a PERT chart than meets the inexperienced eye, and what I hope is that these simple ideas can spark off better ones in your mind, helping you get the most out of your project and non-project plans.

The next chapter ...

... is about corporate cultures. Beware theorists. Orthogonality. Dedication. Effort. Procedures. Language. Satisfaction. Gravity (and lack of it). Dependence. Organisation charts. The world views. Careers. Advice.

Chapter 15: Arranging for a Successful Project Culture

Whenever I hear the word culture
I release the safety catch on my revolver

Hanns Johst

All the World's a Project

This chapter is aimed at the Head Office, the CEO, the department heads as well as the project owners. A question to ask is to what extent is your business in fact a project business? Are you properly organised for carrying out projects? Or are you organised along traditional lines because that's how it's always been? The world about us is replete with evidence of project activity, both from ancient times and post-modern: St. Paul's Cathedral and Canary Wharf, Hadrian's Wall and the M25, Lascaux and the Internet. Apart from nuts, bolts, bananas and mobile phones most of what we see around us is the result of discrete jobs of work, each with a beginning, a middle and an end. We call these jobs of work projects, and over the years we have amassed a wealth of experience in planning and managing them. So much so there can be no excuses today for not making any project reasonably successful – including not doing it at all if the plan says so! Nevertheless, there are still too many failures.

There are reasons for the failures, and lessons to be learned, the most fundamental of which is that few traditional companies, even in today's competitive world, are organised in a way that makes it easy for them to succeed. They may well employ the right kind of people, but they don't support those people with managerial structures appropriate to the task in hand; they don't run project-orientated organisations. Their senior levels of management are not project-minded, and their boardrooms are populated largely by ladder-climbers – not all of whom may be able to earn an honest penny cleaning windows. They may well recognise that they have projects on their hands, but they don't take cognisance of this in their corporate structure, with the consequence that they all too often miss their targets and could therefore be a lot more profitable.

I have spent over five decades in the project world, in both commerce and academia. I have had the privilege of working in the aircraft, the computer, the offshore and the educational industries, as well as the United Nations and the Admiralty. During this time, I have come to realise that there are two distinct forms of corporate animal, the Neolithic farmer and the Palaeolithic hunter, as described by Sir Antony Jay in his book, Corporation Man[13]. The world needs them both, but they must cohabit their territories in a mutually benevolent way. The world needs the former to run the structures of the organisations that together make up our civilisation and the latter to work within those structures to create the physical details. The former is concerned with the law, contracts, finance, facilities, public relations, etc. while the job of the latter is that of designing, building and maintaining the roads, bridges, factories, warehouses and mobile phones that inhabit the modern world.

Their Board Rooms are Populated largely by Ladder-Climbers

A project organisation differs fundamentally from the traditional organisation, and this chapter explains the difference.

Beware Samson, the Theorists are Upon Thee

The problem with the content of many management textbooks is that their authors haven't done the necessary years of experience, or if they have, it is restricted to working in a traditional department rather than on projects.

Most active management is the management of projects and most of the value of the companies in which we work is created by projects. We who spend most of our time in the world of projects know this, but we are too busy working nights and weekends to tell anybody. So the message doesn't get through, and university departments carry on telling their students about how to survive in the corporate jungle, how to get promoted and wind up with an index-linked pension, instead of telling them about the wonderful world of getting things done. But

---

[13] Published by Jonathan Cape (1972)

what does it matter? It matters because we need the best people as project managers. If the youngsters build up a picture of industry and commerce as painted by the theorists they will run away and drive mini cabs, take extended gap years or assume the only thing that matters is the size of their pay packet and their bonus. If this is the case we will lose the best people from the money-earning end of business. Moreover, it matters because the top management of most of the companies I have had anything to do with don't understand the difference and consequently make dreadful though avoidable mistakes, and sadly I am sure they're typical. A proper understanding of the nature of the world of projects would make an enormous difference to the general world in which we work.

Corporate Orthogonality

> *Old Norman's Certainty Principle* **says that if you can see the one you can't see the other**

So we project folk need to explain to our staff colleagues what projects are all about and we need to start by telling them something that isn't easy to understand, that the project world is at right angles to the staff world. It is as though if the traditional structure of companies is in a mathematical sense real, then the project world is imaginary. Or if staff is vertical, project is horizontal. Or if staff is crystalline, project is amorphous. Or if staff is matter, project is antimatter. *Old Norman's Certainty Principle* says that if you can see the one you can't see the other.

Focus

You cannot manage both a department and a project. It has to be one or the other. Each requires your undivided dedication, and experience shows that each requires a very different type of manager of different personal chemistries. And as an associated supplementary, although it is not impossible to manage more than one project at a time, if the projects are of any substantial size it can be very difficult to do so.

You will inevitably meet yourself at the door

But if you do embark upon the hazardous path of undertaking more than one at a time you will inevitably meet yourself at the door and will need a very clear understanding of the relative priorities of the projects. But in practice priorities vary with whom you talk to, the weather and the incidence of sunspots.

Effort

In most companies, most management effort, in terms of man-hours, is project management rather than department management. Moreover, the fact of life is that most projects get well behind schedule, involving the manager and the team in substantial overtime, both at night and weekend. You may not get many staff managers to agree with you, but the fact of life is that project work is far more demanding of time and energy than staff work. Project managers spend much more time on the job than department managers. Department management revolves around the tick-tock of office opening and closing hours. There's no office clock in the project; the project manager goes home when the task is complete. A project manager can never guarantee his family that he'll be around at the weekend. Indeed, it is often the case that project work lies geographically distant from home and a person may be away for long periods of time, in which case he will work long days and weekends. There may not be much else to do, and it gets the job done sooner – or reduces the delay! It's the department managers and board members who clog up the M25 each morning and evening.

**It's the department managers and board members
who clog up the M25 each morning and evening**

Procedures and Lack Thereof

Department management is largely procedural, much of it written down. Staffs tend to evolve steady-state ways of doing things; they work as much as possible to a regular pattern. This enables department managers to adopt an exception mode of operation. As long as things take place according to the procedures, the manager has little to do. As long as he has hired a competent team there will be few exceptions for him to take care of. The successful staff manager can be spotted a mile away, hands in pockets with nothing to do – and rightly so – or attending management conferences (about department management!). Everything is delegated. Project management, on the other hand, is largely creative: task definitions change by the minute as discoveries are made.

┌─────────────────────────────────────┐
│   **Volatility rules!**   │
└─────────────────────────────────────┘

There may be a lot of project documentation (and there may not), but little of it is concerned with the actual management of the project itself. Most project documentation consists of contractual agreements, drawings, manuals, plans, progress reports, variation orders – and the task diary. How the project deliverables shall be produced is very much up to the manager and the individuals doing the work, and during the life of the project there is little opportunity for evolving anything approaching a steady state; volatility rules!

Department managers have trouser pockets and attend
management conferences.
Project managers ride bicycles, megaphone in hand.

The Linguistic Problem

Department management consists largely of working with people of like kind; departments are very largely homogeneous, speaking a common tongue. Project management consists almost entirely of working with people from widely different disciplines, where the manager is a specialist at most in one – and often none at all – getting by with a Babel-fish in his ear. Project management is therefore much more difficult than department management and attracts people who seek challenge.

Department managers are shepherds.
Project managers are Noah trying to save the flood of animal speak.

Satisfaction

Department activity goes on for ever. Project activity ceases when the object has been delivered and the bills settled. The completion of an object – a bicycle, a statue, a symphony, a book, a ballet or a drug is a source of satisfaction that departments simply do not have. Department management in itself doesn't provide much basis for work satisfaction. Instead, it needs substitutes in the form of company politics, personal promotion, salary, perks and the hope of a golden parachute.

The world of the project lacks any sense of gravity

Project managers should of course be well rewarded. Indeed, if the value of the company is primarily the value of the projects, the project managers should have the lion's share of the salary budget and the bonuses (if only!). Promotion on the other hand is virtually non-existent in the project world. Indeed, it is meaningless. While staff organisations have a very clear direction – upwards, project departments don't. There is no up or down; the world of the project lacks any sense of gravity. What is there to be promoted to other than project manager? Once you are there, it is only a question of moving on to another project at the end of the current one. Indeed, after managing one project, you can easily become a subordinate resource on another – and perhaps you should. The born project worker understands this and isn't over bothered with titles or position.

The department world is decorated with wallpaper.
The project world is paved with Task Completes – bikes,
books and ballets.

Dependence

When department managers are away departments go on running, that's what makes it possible to hold all those management conferences. In contrast, projects stop without their project manager. Projects very quickly fall apart if the manager isn't around. Companies are far more dependent on their project managers than their department managers. A good department manager should be able to absent himself from the daily running to attend to other things, self-improvement, company-improvement and making speeches to the chamber of commerce.

**Projects very quickly fall apart
if the Project Manager isn't around**

However good a project manager may be, he must be in the immediate vicinity of the project. Experience shows that too much can go wrong and quickly for the manager to be absent for long.

**Department managers can allow their staff to get on with the job.
Project management is the job.**

The Company Organisation Chart

The document of least value in any organisation is the picture of what the organisation is supposed to look like. There are several reasons for this:-

> The current chart is out of date anyway, and is at best an attempt at describing the previous version but one.
>
> It doesn't tell you how decisions are made; *it is not the influence chart.*
>
> It doesn't tell you what's going on, who is doing it, etc; *it is not the project chart.*
>
> In particular, the higher up the chart you are, the less likely you are to be put on a project.

Yet it is the document that gets produced whenever you introduce someone to a company. One can only conclude that it is a deliberate attempt at obfuscation.

If you really want to know about a company ask instead to see their project plans. These will tell you all you need to know.

If you're thinking of a move don't go near a company that can't put its fingers on its project plans at a moment's notice. They may not want to show them to you, but at least they can wave them in the air.

A Departmental View of the World

To the department manager projects are merely irritants to an otherwise peaceful life. He can't get anything done because his people keep getting hijacked by the project managers. Again, this is a slight caricature. But it is in the best interests of the departments that their employees are frequently on loan to the project teams, out there working on income-bearing tasks, bringing back with them an updated view of the world they have to serve.

**The essential irony is that it is the department manager who
is least in touch with the real world; all is anecdotal.**

A Project View of the World

In the project world the functional departments are merely suppliers of the resources needed to man the projects and guarantors of the quality of those resources. When an employee has no real work to do, he may sit in his department; actors resting between plays. This again is a bit of a caricature, of course. No one sits around doing nothing, and it is in the best interests of the project world that their resources have time to improve their minds and update themselves professionally.

**When you've just come off a project read a book – or
better still write one!**

The Multiple Boss Problem

The essential project/department conflict is the problem of who is your boss? A person seconded from a staff, working on, say, three projects has four bosses. Who's supposed to do what and when? Who decides the priorities? Who gives him his pay raises? (What raises?) Where do his loyalties lie? There are no stock answers to these questions, however their existence must be recognised and dealt with at the onset.

A clue to a healthy project organisation is the existence of a Project Office, to which all the project workers report while away from their home departments. (See Chapter 16.)

Careers, the Avoidance thereof

Staff departments are created as spatial hierarchies, providing paths for careers for their inhabitants and guarantees of eventual Peterisation - overextension beyond one's limit of competence. One is paid according to one's position as opposed to one's value, even to that of Sirdom and even Lordliness. Whereas project teams are created as temporal structures, not spatial. When a project reaches completion it disappears from the corporate picture, and eventually from memory, and the manager has nowhere to go but the next project.

**A clue to a healthy project organisation
is the existence of a Project Office**

The project manager hopes there is one! (There aren't many antiquated project managers in the House of Lords.) The problem with getting to the top of a hierarchy is that you become a vulnerable target for efficiency hunters and you worry about the mismatch between responsibility and competence – how can you continue to fool all of the people all of the time?! No one's an exception to the Peter Principle. This worry causes you to shed your hair and acquire stomach ulcers.

Project managers, on the other hand, are allowed to be born again, each and every time they complete a project. But they are born again with increased experience; every project reveals new ways of getting it wrong; new mistakes to make from which to benefit and thereby increase your value. A project manager is therefore worth more and more the longer he continues and the more mistakes he survives. Department managers' funerals are attended by immortal project managers.

> **While departments outlive their managers,**
> **projects have limited lives and project**
> **managers live to fight again**

The New Organisation

Everybody tells you to change your organisation, especially people who get paid for doing so. But you don't have to create a radically new organisation to take cognisance of the foregoing. Your management consultants have done that to you enough times already, for this, that and the other reason – and often for no reason at all.

All it takes is some modest renaming – plus one new box. Just do the following and you will reap the benefits:-

> **Rename** the VPs, project owners. Their job from now on is to own the projects mounted by the company. Ownership requires and confers authority, responsibility and accountability, including that of providing the budget and acting as the project champion at the political level.
>
> **Put** all the support functions, Accounting, Advertising, Legal, etc. into a Company Services department.

Put all the front-line disciplines, Engineering, Manufacturing, Computing, Communications, etc. into a Resource Suppliers department.

Create the one new box, the Project Office (or Programme Office) responsible for the management of the projects, the computer substrate, project time-sheets, data acquisition, training, etc. If you focus your attention on getting this box right, the rest will fall into place effortlessly. Indeed, if you make the Project Office the core of your corporate structure the rest will fall into place peacefully and you'll have an organisation that works. This is so easy. You'd think it was the core of any management course. But you'd be wrong. But why you'd be wrong is one of the fundamental mysteries of the world of management. If you ever solve it, please let me be the first to know.

Create and promulgate a project Salary Structure. The difficulty to start with will be the lack of a vertical chart to go by. This will force you to think about the true value of people as opposed to their perceived value. And this may fluctuate as the company's fortunes fluctuate. To handle this you might draw a parallel with the army, you could have acting and substantive ranks; majors acting as colonels during the life of a vital battle, reverting to a major's salary when it was over. And whatever you do always ask yourself, are they really worth less than me?

The second best thing to do with an organisation is nothing; just live with it.
The best is let it evolve slowly in true Darwinian style.

Finally advice

The top man: Don't ignore history. The top man in any organisation needs to be an Augustus or a Bismark: someone with a deep understanding of the nature of projects, though not necessarily with any experience of running one. But don't bend over backwards and appoint a Napoleon, someone who only knows projects but with no understanding at all of structures. A Napoleon will, at best, give you a series of successful projects terminated by a disaster. Goodbye France. Goodbye company! By definition, if you get the top man right the rest will follow.

Senior management: Sadly most discussions of company goals, threats, opportunities, fiscal matters, organisation and so on are restricted to the department managers and ignore the project managers. There are several reasons for this: the possible absence of project managerial names from the charts, their prolonged absences from the corridors of power, out there in the world creating profit for the company, their understandable irritation at what they may regard as fruitless chit chat, their lack of involvement in company politics, to name but some.

Ignore your project managers at your peril: It is they who indeed know best what the company should be doing, who should be rewarded, promoted, etc, because it is they who are in closest contact with the customers and the real world. Any healthy discussion of company direction should include the project people telling the staff what they need, and the staff finding out how to supply it.

Project Manager Employees: don't bother with career paths and stay well away from the staff organisation chart. They acquire new experience all the time and steadily increase their true value. To be a successful project worker, keep your talents portable. Stick to the merry-go-round of life, not the ladder. Stay employable. Life is about working. Feel alive! Have fun! But always remember Kevin Keegan: "I'm not the man for the job." If you're good you don't have to take it as there will be another job around the corner. The project management industry is always looking for good people.

A final thought: If you want to be a general stay away from the battlefield, but if you want to win a medal stay away from Whitehall.

The next chapter ...

... describes the all important Project Office, what it is and how to create it. Turf wars. The Project Review group. Evolution. Documentation. Popularity (again). The corporate microscope. And the ubiquitous Fred.

Chapter 16: Establishing a Project Office

A man who has no office to go to is a trial

George Bernard Shaw

An Ecological Intrusion

This chapter is for everyone from the project manager all the way to the top. However, anyone can read it and do what it suggests. It is a free world, as you will see.

In Chapter 15, I opined that the key to the successful implementation of a project culture in an organisation is the creation of a Project Office or Programme Office, responsible for the managing of the projects, the computer substrate, project timesheets, data acquisition, training, etc. And if you get this box right, the rest will fall into place effortlessly. Now there's nothing startling about this. The world abounds with such offices today. But what is lacking is a modus operandi, a formula for spawning the process leading to the creation of a fully functional Project Office. Read on.

The Traditional Turf War

It's easy enough to tell people to transmute the organisation from a traditional staff structure to a structure that explicitly tells the world and the employees that this company is primarily a project company; a structure that makes it pretty clear who is responsible for what and, at a high level, how things are done.

It is another matter entirely to disentangle time-honoured departmental relationships and returf the corporate landscape. But to be successful this is what you have to do. The sum total of the company is not about to change; the current version of the corporate jigsaw puzzle is complete, whether we like it or not. It's just that some of the pieces need rearranging, something you can't do with the ones you buy in the shops.

To enable any corporate ecological intrusion a pathway, a change management process, has to be constructed by reshaping some of the constituent pieces. Even possibly all of them. Managers may have to exchange some of their functions in order to do things better, more profitably, but the upshot will be a smoother operation in which it is easier and more fun to work.

A Modus Operandi

So, how do we do it? There are two components to the answer. The first is solving the problem of the reluctance of managers to divest themselves of some of their hard-won authority, and the second is the question of the scope of the Project Office itself. Experience shows that the Project Office discussions can be eternal, expensive but of no value; it is horrendously difficult convincing people of the advantages to them of divesting themselves of some of their traditional control over events. This is quite natural and needs little explanation. "I know what I've got today but you're asking me to trade it in for an ill-defined tomorrow".

> **Project Office discussions can be eternal, expensive but of no value**

To what problems, then, is a Project Office an alleged solution? How can I be certain that it will function? If it goes pear-shaped how do we get the toothpaste back in the tube? You're asking me to replace authority with influence but I don't have a very pretty face. Stand back and take a helicopter view of the company's activities. It's running projects already. Lots of them. Projects are the company's lifeblood; without them the company would not exist.

The war cry goes up. We know our job. Forget it. The protestations will be mostly genuine and must be answered.

Change management is all part of the healthy process of corporate evolution. And that's the key to it all; companies have to evolve. But from what? What does the corporate DNA look like? How deep is the gene pool?

The Stop List

The discussion can be eternal. So stop the talk! Stop the navel-contemplating infinite loop of organisation chart presentations. Stop trying to define what a project is, other than to agree that a project is something that doesn't last for ever[14]. Stop arguing about to whom the Project Office should report. Stop pontificating on the definition of project accounting. Stop fighting over the relative merits of rival project planning software. Press the corporate stop button. Then press another button labelled "the start process" treat it as if it were an embryonic project. Let your bong resound along the corridors.

Cackle doesn't hatch eggs

The great thing about processes is that they define themselves as they go along. And they always come up with surprises. Not only do they generally answer the questions you thought of, they ask and answer questions you couldn't possibly have thought of, simply because you weren't part of it. It's very much like computer programming: it's not until you dig deeply enough in the detail that you discover what the questions really are – and hence the solutions. Cackle doesn't hatch eggs. So cut it. Instead, carry out the following procedure. It works.

How to do it

This section discusses the key points to consider when establishing a Project office.

---

[14] Of course, that could even include the organisation itself, so you should per-haps put a statute of limitations on it; say three years.

Find yourself a champion.

This shouldn't be too difficult. There must be someone somewhere who understands what projects are all about. Why we have them. What project management is all about. Then the problem becomes one of finding resources:

- How to deal with customers.
- How to extract commitments from the staff.
- Where to find expertise that isn't available within the staff.
- How to goad, cajole and bribe people to meet their commitments.
- How to extract documentation from people who can't write.

And so on; the list is endless. But as a last resort, if there does exist a company hierarchy out there totally lacking in project awareness, unwilling to give the responsibility to one of their in-house project managers, they can always hire me for a week or two to get them started.

How to extract documentation from people who can't write

But what sort of background should you be looking for? Engineering? Finance? Maintenance? Contract administration? Computing? A BA or an MBA[15]? The answer is that it simply doesn't matter. Any and all of these can participate in a project. The overriding requirement is a determination to get it all going.

---

[15]   Is an MBA a science or an art? Neither, it is a foreign language!

But supposing you have located your champion, to whom shall he report? Sales – because he has to understand what an awkward bunch the customers are? Finance – because projects are the fiscal lifeblood of the company? Research – because most projects involve an element of the unknown? Again, it simply doesn't matter. Stop all this talking and get on with it. If you keep fairly quiet about it no one is going to suspect you of political shenanigans. All that matters is that your champion's name is Fred.

> **All that matters is that your champion's name is Fred.**[16]

Convene the PRG, the Project Review Group,

The Project Review Group should comprise one representative from each department or key function.

This group should meet at 9.30 on Tuesdays. It has no mandate, no authority, little responsibility and no reporting procedures. On the other hand, the members shall be highly motivated, but if a department doesn't contain a highly motivated employee then it can stay out of the loop until it does. But highly motivated about what? About projects. They need to be fired up at the mention of projects and be well aware of the management's general lack of understanding of the nature and importance of projects, as well as its clear failure to manage them efficiently. But how do you find such people? That's Fred's first job. Let him do it. But if you have found the right man it won't take him long. He already knows who they are. The constituent parts of the PRG already exist in the pub after work. All you're doing is recognising the obvious and sprinkling holy water on it. (But who are you? Are you beginning to see this? Who is this chapter aimed at? What's your role in all this? Good questions! Keep reading.)

Let the PRG have its head.

Don't call them. They'll call you. By week three they will have identified the classes of projects peculiar to your company, their economics, time-scale, where they report in the organisation, whether they have clearly recognised managers, whether they are the subject of formal contracts,

---

[16] Or Frederica. They are interchangeable.

external or internal, and how many different project planning computer systems are in use – if any at all. They will already have uncovered an indescribable mess. They'll regret ever starting, but this step is a project in its own right, with Fred its project manager. Don't worry. They'll see it through. The end of any project is a collection of deliverables, in this case a corporate map of the projects being manned and planned, together with a serious warning about the Damoclean nature of your company.

The end of any project is a collection of deliverables

The projects will be grouped in fairly obvious ways: Customer projects, R&D, Computer, Equipment Installation, Maintenance shut-down projects, etc. Within these classifications will be subdivisions into fiscal magnitude, long and short term, degree of risk, importance to the company etc; a multidimensional spectrum.

The PRG becomes a permanent feature

While Step 3 was a project, ie of limited time, Step 4 is an **event**, a task of almost zero time. It consists of a proclamation: "The PRG is now a permanent feature of the company's landscape having come to the attention of the Important People and having received their unreserved backing." Though few of them yet understand what it's all about.

It is always the case that a permanent feature is the result of a (temporary) project, even though it may not be recognised as such. Indeed, what could be more appropriate than a "Project" project?

The Evolution

OK, so the Project Review Group is now up and running. It has established itself as the company's eyes and ears for project purposes. That's a good start; it's better than what we had before, which was nothing. But it now needs some teeth if it's going to be of any value. It now needs to evolve into the Project Office, and the key to success is evolution. All intrusions into corporate life should be evolutionary, and perhaps the most successful are those which are so natural that they seem to evolve out of navel fluff; woodworms from the woodwork. What you are doing here is giving nature a gentle helping hand, but don't overdo it. Let it simply continue to happen, and when its existence reaches the notice of the top man you congratulate him on his prescience.

> **All intrusions into corporate life should be evolutionary**

But what's it going to do? Is it going to be a permanent talking shop? Or is it going to get operational? If the latter, what is it going to operate? There's a different answer with each company, but the answers have a useful commonality which makes it worthwhile continuing with this chapter.

The one certain common attribute is the creation of project procedures backed up by some simple documentation. Now a fact of life which you have to accept is that project people hate procedures and can't (or don't) write. Bureaucracy is anathema to the creative spirit, and project people are creators[17]. It's no good trying to explain to project managers that the modern world in which they live can only function if it is largely driven by bureaucracy. Their salaries are paid by procedure. Their bank statements are printed and sent by procedure, and so on. But project managers are different. Each day

---

[17]   And here's a fact that the Important People must recognise, that, again, it's the project people more than anyone who create the wealth of the company.

is a brand new adventure. So corporate bureaucracy must have a human face; it must be effortless and inconspicuous. And your people must see an immediate value to it all. The creation of the documents in itself is a revealing exercise, and one step deeper into the detail of the organisation. It's easy enough to create a form to fill in, but is it obvious what it all means? To make sure, the PRG will perforce need to consult a broad spread of company people. And this consultative process will help it acquire credibility and support where it is vitally needed. But what are the documents? What needs to be written, who should write them, who needs them and when?

Documentation

A project is like a game of chess; it has a beginning, a middle and an end. And its middle will consist of much detail. But to start with it has a beginning, so what more natural than a document stating the fact? The PI, the Project Initiation Document. Just this single document, as simple as it might be, is an earth-shattering event. The company now recognises the concept of the project. It admits its existence, and it happens despite the metaphysics of Chapter 1. Furthermore it is accompanied by the Big Bong, for all to hear.

What shall the PI consist of? What do we want to know at the outset? Indeed what is knowable? The project needs a name, a number, today's date, the name of its manager, the owning organisation, the classification (customer, research etc.), the customer's name (external or internal), the venue. But should it also contain the budget and time scale? Can you really know the budget and time scale before you have done some work? And has the PRG manager been appointed yet? The very act of creating a PI brings you immediately onto the iterative and somewhat metaphysical nature of project start up. The idea of a project spawns the PI and the PI catalyses the onset of the project. The rest you can work out for yourself, project by project. And they're all different. You'll learn a lot. (See Chapter 7 for a detailed description of the PI.)

The PI is the document you have no choice but to create. The follow-on documents, the documentary spine of the project, can be evolved according to the nature of the company and the inventiveness of the PRG and its close associates.[18]

---

[18] To hit the deck running you can get some excellent ideas for documentation from two superb books by Mike Watson, "*Managing Smaller Projects: A Practical Approach*" (2006) Multi-Media Publications and "Projects Kept Simple in 90 minutes" (2009) Management Books 2000 Ltd.

It is here where the Project Office rears its head. As the PRG evolves its understanding of project needs and its procedures for supplying those needs, it will inevitably feel the pressure to unify the corporate project world – over everyone's dead body! It will discover a goldmine of opportunity for improving the profitability of the company and it will want to create machinery to do the mining. That machinery is the Project Office, and the remaining question is – of all the things the Project Office could consist of, what should it consist of?

How Big do You Want the Project Office?

The very minimum is a one-man show called Fred. A single person with the full-time responsibility of maintaining a map of the corporate project status is a vast improvement over no one at all. Fred would run the Tuesday morning PRG meeting, write the minutes and circulate them to affected parties, make sure that appropriate computer systems were available, together with the training, know where resources can be found, both internal and contract, and generally give advice where needed, either sought or proffered. Fred needs to be a popular person, remembering that the key to successful management is popularity. Fred needs to be someone you enjoy working with and whom you trust. Indeed, someone who makes a difference!

The key to successful management is *popularity*

The one-man Project Review Group has the wherewithal of being scaled up as experience shows that it has an important role to play and is enhancing the company's profitability.

At the other end of the spectrum, you can transfer many of the traditional responsibilities from the various departments and create an all-bells-and-whistles Project/Programme Command Centre. This would be the beating heart of the company. And at the heart of the heart would be a networked computer system with terminals wherever needed, the key to an HCPS, a Holistic Corporate Project Service. While the several departments may be the owners of the projects, with their project champions acting at the corporate level, the Project Office could be responsible for carrying them out.

What Goes into a Project Office?

A pick list of functions that could be bestowed upon the centre is as follows:

> *The Project Managers:* the home base for the professional project managers, solving a well known problem once and for all. Project management isn't a role that is easily taught, and there is no traditional discipline that produces more project managers than any other. Project managers come from everywhere and perforce have to deal with the total spectrum of disciplines. In this way, with time, they tend to osmose away from their original home and become wanderers. Corral them into the Project Office. Let them sit cheek by jowl with one another and create a new, well-defined discipline. Let them swap yarns between projects and learn from one another.

> *Project resources:* all requirements for people, equipment, materials, facilities to be provided and where the Project Office gets them from is entirely up to the Project Resource team. "Just get them!" is the cry to which they respond. Of course, the traditional departments, Engineering, Manufacturing, Contract Administration, etc. will continue to be the basic suppliers of people and other resources, but only the Project Office is capable of a holistic view. So let the Project Office do the selecting, negotiating and the internal contracting. In this way it will build up a unique view of what the company has got, and will become

acutely aware of what it's missing and what to do about it. And for those bought in solely for the life of the project it gives a single point of entry for outside contractors.

Project viability: all ideas for new projects to be evaluated here, a single point to guarantee uniform financial analysis. By all means let each project owner make his own case, but let the cases be judged uniformly. And if the PRG recommends turning a project down, its proposer has every right to take it up the line. We all learn from corporate fisticuffs.

Project visibility: maintaining wall and screen displays, for example, showing the progress of each of the (major) projects as they pass from stage to stage.

Quality assurance: maintaining a uniform company understanding of quality requirements, carrying out appropriate training of project staff and monitoring project quality for conformity.

Risk management: maintaining a purview of the characteristic risks that are inevitably taken in the course of company business; ensuring that project teams are aware of possible risks and are trained in how to document, monitor and minimise them – or, better still, eradicate them.

Project secretariat: support for project functions as required by individual project managers – planning, reporting, training, contracting, accounting etc.

Computer provision: the debate here can get acrimonious: should you let each project manager use the system he learned five years ago, possibly somewhere else, but is comfortable with? Or should you harmonise? If the latter it would be the Project Office's task to keep a watchful eye on the availability of new project planning systems, keeping up with the state of the art and providing a uniform system throughout the company. My advice, though, is to harmonise. Systems evolve quickly, and integrating the information wherever possible is essential for transparency and must be made a seamless matter.

Corporate reporting: reporting total company project progress to senior management, not least total resource and cash flow aggregation. The project display is, of course, part of the reporting process.

Where Does the Project Office Belong?

The whole point of the Project Office is to make it easy for the company to mount projects. And the way to create it is to let it ooze onto the company landscape from single-celled protozoa evolving into an ever higher form of corporate life, depending on company culture, nature of the business, idiosyncrasies of the people involved and so on. And one of the great benefits of doing it this way is that no one at any stage can destroy it because, hey presto, nobody owns it. It is a horizontal, interdisciplinary animal, just like computing and office cleaning, with a life and a home of its own.

> ### No one at any stage can destroy it because nobody owns it

Eventually, when it has become a de facto part of life, and the top man has taken all the credit, you can argue the toss about where it belongs.

The people most vulnerable to the new arrangement are the project owners. Combine the project owners into a single (virtual) group and let the Project Office report to it. Of course, people aren't project owners all the time, hence the group's virtual nature. You may not be able to draw it on an organisation chart, but it will work because the project owners will want to keep the project managers on a tight lead. This will have a beneficial side effect on the organisation, as it will create synergies between the project owners who hitherto had been operating *in vacuo*.

A nuance to this is appointing a Programme Manager, with the Project Office reporting to him, in which case it would become the Programme Office.

There are other arguments for where it shall report but who cares as long as it works?

The Corporate Microscope

There is a final point to be made to any managing director who may perchance be reading these lines. The Project Review Group is a wonderful corporate microscope. It throws the spotlight on the critical problems surrounding the company. If the company is the sum total of its projects then the project issues are precisely those details that the top man should want to know about more than any other. If he drops in on the PRG meetings, not to take part but to listen, he will learn a lot.

> **The Project Review Group is a wonderful corporate microscope.**

He will learn much more than he does at his departmental meetings. Unfortunately, it is rare to meet a managing director who has much love for corporate detail; most run a mile when a deep down detail raises its ugly head. Not so the Duke of Wellington.

And What About Fred?

Ah yes, but what about you? Who are you? How did you get here? The fact is you're just anybody. You just happened to be born with project genes and you'd like to be a hero. So go ahead Fred, it's all yours.

Fred going ahead

The next chapter ...

... is about management and leadership, two very different qualities. Staff and projects. Churchill and Atlee. Orthogonality (again). Genes. Language (again). Two world views (again). Careers (again). Identity. And, above all, heroism.

Chapter 17: Management vs. Leadership – Staff vs. Projects

A leader whose eloquence and experience are indispensable to them

Macaulay

A Little Philosophy

This chapter is for everyone to read: the apprentice with a general manager's knapsack on his back to the chairman of the board worrying what to spend his bonus on. This chapter will not help you much to run projects, at least directly. However, it should help you find the right people to undertake the multiplicity of tasks that the project world requires. It is based entirely on years of experience and management theory gained from observation, if such can be said to exist. If you don't agree with it, at least arguing about it might help clear your mind and crystallise your own experience.

This chapter is about managers and leaders, something you might have thought were two words for the same thing.

Management vs. Leadership, Staff vs. Projects

Managers and leaders are indeed very different specimens of humanity, though you wouldn't know it from the literature. This chapter is aimed to redress this situation, to explain the differences with crystal clarity and to help you decide whether you are the one or the other (or even neither). I have known superb managers and inspirational leaders. I have built up and managed departments, spawned and managed projects. I've made the mistakes, and watched others make them and by now I have amassed enough evidence to understand the differences.

I know where I belong. The following is to help you make up your own mind as to where you belong.

An Historical Precedent

Perhaps a good way of getting the discussion about managers and leaders started is to name names; if you want to talk leadership, start at the top. In the recent past, we have been blessed with at least one superb example of an outstanding leader and an outstanding manager, Churchill and Attlee.

Can one imagine Lord Halifax or Anthony Eden exhorting us to fight 'em on the beaches?

If ever this country has needed a leader it was in 1940, and it is a spine-chilling thought to recall how close we came to not appointing Churchill Prime Minister. Can anyone imagine Lord Halifax or Anthony Eden exhorting us to fight 'em on the beaches? If leadership in Churchill's case consisted of no more than the speeches it would have been enough; for what seemed like infinity at the time he was our only weapon. The British people were all under the impression that Churchill was managing the war effort. And that was a good thing; they thought that there was a direct connection between the speeches and the actions; they thought he was the manager. He wasn't. We learned about this when it was all over.

What actually happened was that he appointed Lord Alanbrooke to do the managing and Alanbrooke's job started right there at the top – managing Churchill, a most unrewarding, though necessary, task. The rest of it was managing the manifold detail of the war effort, whatever it might be from hour to hour.

Then when it was all over, we said thank you very much for the leadership bit Sir Winston, but we now need a manager in charge, Clement Attlee. Britain was in a post-war mess and it needed a systematic manager to clean it all up. No speeches thank you; no heroics; a good Cabinet chairman; attention to detail; thorough follow-up; clear understanding of the vision; able to delegate without interfering; good grasp of finance. And so on.

Human Orthogonality

Churchill was a project man but he had a solid staff man at his side in Lord Allenbrooke.

Attlee was a staff man, but he had excellent project men at his side when it came his turn to run things, not least Aneurin Bevan who created the National Health Service.

And there's the clue. As we said in Chapter 17, project and staff components are two orthogonally different structures. And they are populated by two orthogonally different manifestations of *Homo sapiens*, the hunter and the camper, the team player and the organiser.

It's in the Genes (at least most of it is)

Most of us have elements of both in our makeup, but each individual is more one than the other.

> **We can all take violin lessons**

And I believe that it lies deeply in our genes. Training does little to bend an individual from the one to the other. We can all take violin lessons, but not many of us become violinists. It's the same with carpentry, watch repairing and mathematics. We can read the books and attend the lectures but without the genes we don't get far; we are born project folk or we're born organisation folk – or perhaps we're not born either and leave such things to others. You don't have to be a manager. There are plenty of other things to do in life.

The Spectrum of Organisations

From the project point of view there is a spectrum of organisations from those whose sole task is to mount projects to those who mount none at all. In the former case, the staff is simply a mechanism for spawning projects.

The staff groups will be almost skeletal

The added value of the company is the work carried out by the project teams. Typically, in terms of manpower most employees will be assigned to project teams, while the staff groups will be almost skeletal, confined to the role of management, sales, finance, resource acquisition and general support activities. A typical organisation chart will depict the staff functions but not the projects.[19] It may show a Project Office, a support function that provides project tools such as the computer system and training, but the detailed manning and progress of projects are not features that are easily or appropriately displayed in an organisation. For one thing, they are too transitory. People move from project to project as needed. But more importantly, very rarely are project managers selected from amongst the department managers. And here's the nub: this is where we find the essential difference between the leader and the manager. Although his title is project manager, he is a *leader* by function as well as by nature. It's just a title that's been around for too long to change. Project managers are Antony Jay's[20] hunters. Consider some of the problems their job involves:-

---

[19] Though see chapter 8
[20] Corporation Man, (1972) by Sir Antony Jay

Language: The head of the electrical engineering department is an electrical engineer. His language is replete with volts, amps and circuits, as is that of his subordinates, some of whom may stem from Outer Mongolia and not speak very good English, but they are welded by means of their discipline. He has a comfortable relationship with them, and his main task is that of hiring them, ensuring their continuous training and assignment to projects as required. The project manager, on the other hand, is not necessarily a specialist at any of the disciplines involved in his current project and may not have a technical language in common with any of them. He is welded to his team by means of the prize at the end of the hunt. A manager is a detail person, a leader paints the broad picture and communicates by means of the pictures on the cave wall.

Procedures: Staffs are virtually permanent structures and work according to company standards and procedures. Time is on their side; the investment of time and effort in determining the relationships between the organisation boxes is worth it. It is these relationships that enable the smooth flow of corporate life; it is the CEO's way of moulding company culture and *modus operandi*. Projects, on the other hand, are not objects amenable to long-term procedures. They may well evolve temporary agreements to get through the next critical phase, but each task is usually a brand new hunting experience. They have no time or need to talk about how to do things. They just do them. They can chat about them in the pub afterwards but right now they'll tackle today's problems today; there's only a short-term tomorrow to invest in.

Effort: Running a staff department is a steady-state, nine to five operation – as it should be. It isn't healthy to work erratic hours; it is not conducive to steady professional and corporate growth. Steady state is symptomatic of the lifestyle of the staff manager. Not so the project manager. Overhanging every project is an inevitable series of Damoclean swords, brought about by a combination of contractual fog, difficulty of estimating the inestimable, underestimating technical difficulty etc. This guarantees an atmosphere of adventure and uncertainty in a project, the essence of the leader's life. That's what hunting's all about. Moreover, projects often involve working away from home where there's nothing much to do at weekends, so everyone works. Staff managers have peaceful nights and weekends, which atone for the dull nature of the job. In contrast to the leader, whose life is work. The buzz is its own reward.

An inevitable series of Damoclean swords

The Two World Views

More generally, to the project world the job of the Functional Departments is to supply the projects with its resources and to guarantee their quality. The organisation is a melange of boxes whence people come when needed and where they return when it's all over, to rehabilitate, to read, to write, to spread corporate learning and to sharpen their wits and their spears for the next hunt. To the staff the caricature of the project world is that of a constant irritant to an otherwise peaceful life as people are borrowed to man the hunting parties.

Careers

Each individual has to decide where he fits into the eventual scheme of things; where he feels at home. If promotion and position are the spur, stay in your box. Your chances of becoming CEO are far better if you are constantly seen in the corridors, your name on progressively loftier boxes on the chart. This is the managerial route to the index-linked pension. Company boards appoint safe pairs of hands to the head shed; people they know. A project career can be a very shaky ride.

However, it could be said that the top staff job is the Managing Director. But what about the Chairman or Research Director? The Chairman is a leader and so most likely is the Research Director. Their DNA will be different to that of the Managing Director. Deep down they will be project managers at heart. The problem is there is no established career path for outstanding project managers to leap to the top of an organisation. Unless, and here is a new thought, Fred as chairman of the Project Review Group is elevated to the board. He would loathe the tedium of board meetings, but the PRG needs a voice and Fred will have valuable things to say as a board member or, later, even as its Chairman.

> **A true leader must be willing to be led**

Being a project manager (i.e. leader) one year is no guarantee of being a project manager the next. A project manager is merely *primus inter pares* for the time being – a most temporary state of affairs. Project dwellers are recyclable. A true leader must be willing to be led. Position must be a temporary phenomenon. When the project is over there's no guarantee that there will be another one just waiting for you. Life isn't like that, and your spur must be the technical fun that the project provides.

However, an astute project-based organisation should place a high value on good project managers because without projects the company will not prosper. Someone in management should have the task of liaising with the PRG to identify lulls in the project workflow and plan carefully to minimise such times. A temporary solution could be to build sabbaticals into their employment contract.

Fred - A Corporate Asset

Had Lewis Carol been alive today he would probably have had a lot of fun writing satires of the Wonderlands of Companies, even though many companies are satires in their own right. In particular, he might have described their propensity to reorganise themselves to something approaching an ants' nest. This, of course, is amplified by the worshipful academy of consultants. Their source of survival is the concept of change, and their slogan is *plus ça change, plus c'est la meme chose*. The more often their clients change their *modus vivendi*, the deeper the consultants' pockets. And to catalyse change they employ one of the modern management techniques, Change Management. Now, if you're going to move stuff and staff around you should do it properly, and should adopt change management in the project management sense. But until you have completed the change and had it running for three years you cannot be certain that it will work. Did they remember to install enough power outlets? Was the door wide enough to get the equipment in? Was the outsourcing to Asia what the customers wanted? Has some small but essential cog in the organisation been discarded, and so on?

And it is here that the Project Office can be brought to bear as an unexpected asset. The one point about the PRG and Fred is that the former was allowed to grow in a totally unplanned manner. In the process thereof, Fred will have acquired some very valuable and unpurchasable experience, which he could use to help the change management team do its job. Fred's process was not managed, it was allowed to evolve naturally, and it survived; it stood the test of viability. Practical experience might remind the change management team of something they had omitted.

Ah, but the Ultimate Project Career Move

Although it doesn't lie in the genes of most project folk to rise to the top of anything, there is an ultimate step that could provide a late career move for a project manager. This step could be seen as a reward for a successful life in the hurly-burly of company activity as well as the solution to the problem of finding good board chairmen. We said earlier that the general manager should be something like 80% manager and 20% leader; enough of a leader to be able to spot good leaders for his projects.

Sadly, there are far too many top level companies in which it is difficult to tell the CEO and the chairman apart. Both are experienced managers, and the only difference between them is that leadership has been thrust on the chairman's shoulders late in his career.

The top staff job is that of Managing Director; no discussion. But, in the main, the safe pairs of hands who populate his board are also MDs of other companies or retired MDs. Suddenly you ask, but where's the leadership at the top? Why not put a super successful project manager right there where he can run the entire company as a project? Invert the internal relationship between the two and think of it historically. The company started as a project: some creative person had a great idea and from the intimacy of his garage he started to implement that idea; why not keep it that way? The project started the day he took up residence in the garage and ended the day he employed his first accountant: the day on which the company excitement vanished. On the way he hired engineers and computer folk, graphic designers and crane operators, all professionals, but abdicated the financial stuff to his cousin or wife.

But the day their first delivery was made, the day they moved from the garage to the empty offices down town, something vanished from the scene. I have seen it so many times. People's days start to shorten, they stop showing up at the weekend. No more burning midnight oil and no more lunchtime darts. The company instigator is eventually moved aside to make room for a professional manager, and something happens to the *esprit de corps*.

Of course, once the market place has taken the company seriously, and customers and shareholders have emerged, it is only good business sense to mirror them spiritually and in appearance. But it shouldn't be done to the detriment of the creative spirit. So, to counteract the consequences of the traditional managerial superstructure, appoint an experienced project manager as chairman of the board, in which position he can inject creative leadership from above. And give him an office in the building. He is not operational; he can't tell anyone what to do, but he can wander the corridors and ask all the right questions he likes and make all the suggestions. He could close the loop between the messenger boy and the House of Lords.

Fred may well loathe the tedium of the board meetings, but the PRG needs a voice and Fred will have valuable things to say. Board meetings will no longer be confined to profitability but to how that profitability can be achieved.

This brings us back to where we started the chapter. The Atlees of this world have become the predominant force in big company culture. They are content to close down the career paths of the Wellingtons and Churchills, whose DNA has not made them suitable for the long slog up the corporate staff ladder. Organisations led by managers at best seek to maintain the status quo. Over time they go the way of the dinosaur: the takeover, the bailout[21] followed by insolvency. It may take years in coming but the seeds of decline are sown right at the appointment of the leaderless Board.

Dependence

Staff departments run themselves. As we have said, ad nauseam, when department managers are away departments go on running. Project teams don't. Projects very quickly fall apart if the leader isn't around. Where's the plan? What are we supposed to be doing? Where's old Charlie? Did he find his wheelbarrow? A good staff manager should be able to absent himself from the daily running to attend to other things, self-improvement, company improvement and making speeches to the chamber of commerce. However good a project manager may be, he must be in the immediate vicinity of the project. Experience shows that too much can go wrong too quickly for the project manager to be long gone. Indeed, this problem is a fundamental reason why the concept of project figures so little in the managerial educational world.

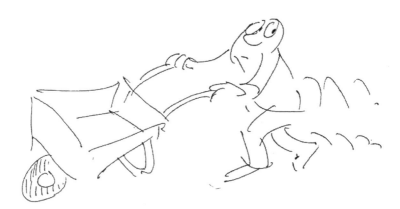

Did Charlie find his Wheelbarrow?

---

[21] Or perhaps they are not too big to fail and there is no bailout.

Identity

Management is an amorphous substance as opposed to the crystal clarity of leadership. It is very difficult for a department manager to be identified with a specific product; his working life and responsibilities are spread over everything the department gets involved in. Department managers are often not focussed on anything in particular. His visible output consists of lines, boxes, numbers and words on bits of paper, all related to the diverse activities carried out by his company, but he is not directly involved in them.

On the other hand, the project manager becomes identified with the subject of his project, for good or ill: old Bill's Bridge, old Tom's Tower Block – and even old Fred's Fudge down in the bowels of the London Underground. Even I have had my moment of fame – the school cabin-painting disaster project. The paint can and the waffle mixture bowl were standing side by side on the playground table and I failed to distinguish between the two. When I had finished the painting, the good lady PTA chairperson, and schoolyard manager, became incandescent, but though it was reported in the local paper, after all this time nobody thankfully remembers who dunnit.

Heroism

Every organisation needs heroes. No heroes, no soul, no purpose, no culture; no corporate glue; all stations to instability, stagnation and failure. Heroes are not only the people who get things done, they are seen to get things done; they are identified with their victories.

So stemming from the previous section, heroism can only come from projects; battles fought and battles won. In my days at Boeing we had heroes, the greatest of which was one Tex Johnson, the chief test pilot. He rolled the first ever 707, the Dash-80, over the annual boat race on Lake Washington and a crowd of a hundred thousand people lining the lake shore, all of whom spontaneously ducked. He flew it like a four-engined Spitfire, something it was certainly not designed to be. With people of that calibre everyone worth his salt wanted to work for Boeing and they streamed in from all over the world to be part of the mid-century technology boom that ushered in the age of universal air travel. It was this optimism that led Harold Wilson, when he became Prime Minister, to browbeat British industry into harnessing the fruits of modern technology in the workplace.

A not-unimportant consequence of having a Pantheon of Olympian heroes is the feeling at lower staff levels that even if the calibre of your immediate manager isn't of inspirational magnitude it doesn't matter; it's still a good place to work right now, and the prospects for the future are exciting.

The View From the Top

The healthy company is the company in which there is a constant rivalry between staff and project, managers and leaders. The successful CEO is he who reigns over a perpetual civil war. No fight, no corporate energy. He must see the relationship between the two worlds as a healthy symbiosis. The organisation chart, populated by the managers, is the structure, the human bricks and mortar, the corporate continuity, the market identity.

> **The successful CEO is he who reigns over a perpetual civil war**

On the other hand, the pulsating project teams are the corporate energy, the excitement, the value-creation process, the company's future, its existence. The organisation needs both staff and project expertise to prosper.

The Essential Problem

Many management academics assert that the CEO must have leadership qualities, and I absolutely agree. Leadership qualities, but I don't want him to be a leader. The CEO shall be 80% manager and only 20% leader. The 20% is to ensure that he has one day a week to make the speeches and understands enough about the project function to be able to organise for it. To run the whole caboodle he must be able to delegate everything except his thought processes – and that includes the ability to spot another leader when he sees one.

Next to the CEO is the Chairman. His role is reversed, 80% leader and 20% manager. Put the CEO and Chairman together and one has the management and leadership boxes ticked with 100% in each; the perfect corporate symbiotic relationship.

A Fundamental Flaw Removed

Distinguishing between the two tribal domains of *Homo sapiens* is very much the key to corporate success.

However, this does not have to be the case. The Project Office and the existence of a Project Review Group are fundamental prerequisites if a company seeks to manage its leadership pool. Outstanding leaders coming to the fore in this environment could be weaned into the corporate decision-making structure. Who knows, one of them might be a Chairman one day.

Private vs. Public Sectors

However, it is a very different situation when one considers the massive volume of projects mounted by the public sector. Projects need managers capable of giving their charges hands-on attention. Project teams need people with experience, lots of experience, and an understanding of risk. Projects need what this book is all about. The UK public sector approach to joining the world of projects is to train the civil servants to become project managers.[22] Unless the participants have extensive hands-on project management experience, this won't achieve anything. An analogy is whether you can train people mogul skiing without taking them out on the slopes — I am very doubtful.

A debate has to be had as to how the considerable project expertise that exists in the private sector can be harnessed by the public sector. The Private Finance Initiative (PFI) goes some of the way, but it is predominantly a finance mechanism to push Government borrowings off the national balance sheet.[23]

What is needed is a mechanism for the supervision of public sector projects. The call should go out to find a Fred to start the ball rolling. The fledgling Project Office and Project Review Group should have a channel of communication straight through to the Cabinet Office.

Where there is found to be a skills shortage in the public sector the required project management skills should be brought in or outsourced and not come from training up insiders, unless one is prepared to wait ten

---

[22] Viz, the new Major Projects Leadership Academy (MPLA) for civil servants responsible for major Government projects at Oxford University's Saïd Business School.

[23] In some instances value for money has been achieved, in others the built-in escalators are starting to make PFI projects, in an era of low interest rates, exceedingly expensive, and excellent earners for the banking community.

or more years. Good project managers have a decade or more of project experience; they cannot simply be sent on courses to get their training.

Distinguishing between the two tribal domains of *Homo sapiens* is very much the key to corporate success. However, I do know one exception to this, the CEO of a British aircraft company whose what-if management meetings consist of a real-time review of the total corporate resource availability and allocation picture.[24]

This brings up the discussion of the public versus the private sectors, and the chasm of difference between how the two handle their computer (and possibly other) projects. It all stems from leadership.

At the base of the discussion lies the essential difference between the *raison d'être* of each sector, Public Good versus Profit. The atmosphere, chemistry and so on are so different. Can the twain ever meet? That question is far beyond the scope of this book, but this shouldn't prevent an honest discussion of the managerial differences between the two.

The public sector is run by managers, as is to be expected, but there is little evidence of much leadership in the Civil Service. And, as we have said on countless occasions in this book, there is a big difference between the two. Moreover, the lack of leadership continues right to the top, where the concept of project ownership is utterly absent. The public sector has billons of pounds worth of projects under its belt, no doubt with extensive committees of managers acting as the interfaces between government and the private suppliers, but next to none with technical specialists and project managers in place. In particular, I have never heard of the existence of a project office in any discussion of Whitehall arrangements.

Conclusion

As I have discussed above, I'm convinced that few of our company bosses have enough of the project genes to do as good a job as they should. I see too many companies too ill-equipped to arrange for a healthy project culture. This is particularly dangerous when the role of Chairman and CEO are combined.

---

[24] This review meeting is made possible by some very fancy software footwork, interactive bar charts and histograms. You might find this visible on the Internet at:- www.pcfltd.co.uk/resources/
If, for some reason, this display has been removed, try contacting PCF (see Chapter 18). It is a mind-blowing example of Computer-aided Management.

No symbiosis. But the essence of the problem lies one step away at board level because they are tightly involved in the senior operational appointments. Where do the boards come from? Who appoints them? What is their function? Do company boards have the necessary experience of leadership themselves to appoint managers with sufficient leadership qualities to become viable CEOs? Where does the Chairman come from, and does he have the charismatic leadership skills?

This is a convoluted question lacking any general answer, though when I read the *Financial Times* and *Private Eye* I am not encouraged. What we need are courses along the lines of Project Culture Made Simple for Industrial Leaders. And a recognition that leaders and managers are fundamentally different people. Leaders understand the project culture, the life blood of most companies, while managers understand how to manage staff, keep the company on an even keel and have a major role as the project owners.

And You?

One way of finding out whether you are a leader is standing up in somebody else's meeting and saying, "this is a sheer waste of time, this meeting's over." If the others follow you out you're a leader.

On the other hand, if you compulsively hit the deck running each morning you're a manager. But ultimately it comes down to the question of desks. Managers sit at desks, while leaders don't need desks. They are out there in the project sitting at someone else's desk - or helping them with their wheelbarrow.

The next chapter ...

... describes a company, project-based from the very top. The essence of running the company is planning – from the very top. Evolution of planning systems. Unifying corporate data. The computer as a corporate catalyst.

Chapter 18: Integrated Project Planning at Augusta Westland

You ask me what it is I do. Well actually, you know,
I'm partly a liaison man and partly P.R.O.
Essentially I integrate the current export drive
And basically I'm viable from ten o'clock till five

John Betjeman

A Project-based Company

This chapter is a description of the best project-organised company I have ever encountered. I professed in Chapter 17 that a CEO should be about 80% manager and only some 20% leader; he should ensure that the right things were being done but shouldn't get involved in the doing. In terms of a project-based company I mean that he should have sufficient understanding of project technology to ensure that he has a good project organisation in his company and leave it at that. However, I know of one exception to this, the CEO of an aircraft company whose what-if management meetings consist of a real-time review of the total corporate resource availability and allocation picture. This is the AugustaWestland (AW) helicopter company in Yeovil, Somerset. And as time goes on I see more and more top people taking advantage of today's gee-whiz picture interface and super-zap data transmission to understand what their companies are up to and to participate in the action. The topic of this chapter has two invaluable benefits, that of subliminally educating the boss as well as inviting him to influence the decisions on the fly instead of after they have flown.

Although project management computer systems have been around for over thirty years, catalysing the acceptance of project management as a profession and project organisation as a way of life in companies, very few companies have come very far in this evolutionary process. However AugustaWestland today may well be the sole exception, but a lot can be learned from their story.

Still today, many companies that are primarily project-orientated in their work are nevertheless still organised on a staff-and-line basis, and have computer systems geared, vertically, around the organisation as opposed to horizontally around the work. This chapter is an explanation of how AW has evolved to where it is today, starting from the very early days of electronic computing. It is a fascinating story with broad applicability throughout industry, and it is time somebody broadcast the fact. It is as shining an example of how the boss of a project-based company should do his job as any I have encountered.

The Role of Planning

AW is a global manufacturer of helicopters, with connections with companies in the USA, Europe and Japan. All sales are based on individual contracts: no "white-tail" hopefuls – helicopters sitting on the runway awaiting a customer and a pot of paint. Thus all business is project-based, of long project lifetime, few at a time.

> **Red-end boards can earn their money!**

Planning is the life-blood of AW and it all starts where the textbooks say it should start, at the point of sales. But in a sense this is a fairly obvious and easy idea at a company like AW in that it is a company with few individual sales – few but, of course, very large. Whereas many, perhaps most, companies sell shoes and ships and sealing wax, from catalogues, each sale a microscopic component of the whole, many sales per day, AW makes one sale at a time at perhaps a rate of one per year. If Tesco and M&S are at the blue, high-frequency end of the sales spectrum, AW is at the red, long wave length, low frequency end. Moreover, while the blue-end companies have to content themselves with statistical reports at boardroom meetings, blurring their view of company detail, at the red end a board meeting can be confronted with accurate pictures of today's stark reality and various versions of tomorrow's aspirations. A red-end board can focus its attention on time bar charts and resource histograms, understand them, ask what-if questions and get instant, honest answers. They can behave like project managers. Red-end boards can earn their money!

Getting the Software Right

But it hasn't always been that way. We need a little history to reveal the evolutionary process. One place to start would be to tell an incredulous world that the planning was done using Microsoft's Excel system. But Excel doesn't contain a calendar, so it cannot be a planning device – which of course it isn't. In reality it is a device for displaying the results of planning. To a limited extent the Microsoft Project (MSP) planning system uses Excel for its graphical output, and AW originally used MSP to produce dates, which were then transcribed to Excel; they did it backwards. This process took some four weeks per shot. Wonderful artistry, but very expensive, time-consuming and far from interactive, so consideration was made of writing a program to automate the data transcription from MSP to Excel. But instead they looked around to find a system that would do the trick, and happily they found one, QEI, a project management system from PCF Ltd.[25]

The Evolution of Planning Systems

Planning of any sort is a combinatorial problem. That is to say, it involves the interaction of large numbers of factors, each often very large, and certainly too large for the unassisted human brain to handle. If you've ever had to wrestle with the details of the timetable of a simple school you will enthusiastically agree. Miss Smith's aged mother has to be taken to the clinic every Thursday morning. Year 9 have French five mornings a week. Miss Smith teaches Year 9 French. This problem, in many guises, crops up all over the place, and school timetabling programs are horrendously difficult to write – as are all scheduling programs. But what they replace is even worse.

I discovered this in 1958 when I wrote my first scheduling program. It scheduled the oil in the two-thousand mile long pipeline from Edmonton, Alberta, to Toronto. There were six different grades of "sweetness" (sulphur content) and each refinery along the line was built specifically to handle one and only one type. The line contained two months' oil, all of which had to be delivered to specific refineries. The scheduling department in Edmonton had a staff of ten people, whose job was primarily to ensure that the batches of oil arrived at the right places on time. But oil refineries have fires and strikes, as well as minor breakdowns, except for the fact that the adjective "minor" doesn't exist in the petroleum industry's vocabulary.

---

[25] Website: www.pcfltd.co.uk

Scheduling the oil pipeline across Canada was probably easier than most other examples, but it was difficult enough, and anyway it cost money. My job was to move it over to a computer of, by definition, very early vintage. Nevertheless, when the program was finished the run time was only four minutes. Even though it was by today's standards very slow it essentially removed the scheduling problem – which had an undreamed of advantage. Though the company could plan a month's deliveries in a month, they didn't have a month in which to reschedule deliveries whenever a catastrophe occurred. But they did have the four minutes. Planning is enough of a problem, but replanning is really serious stuff.

Since that time development was inexplicably slow, and it took another twenty years before things started to move, and even then there seems to have been a reluctance on the part of large companies to make profitable use of the systems on offer. The exception to this has been the offshore petroleum sector with younger people handling an expensive commodity.

Nevertheless, when Excel became available, with its easy-to use output facilities, people started to use it in conjunction with their traditional hand methods. The output was handled by the computer, but the actual planning was still done by hand. Not really what the planners wanted, but at least it brought the computer into the planning office.

In terms of generations of software development, the program, QEI, is perhaps the first of the third generation of project planning computer systems. The first generation came about during the punched-card, batch-processing era up to about 1979; calculator-friendly, and better than wall charts, but still involving a lot of human intervention. Then came the second-generation interactive era, with systems such as Artemis and Primavera, as the second, producing screen pictures of networks and bar charts; all very planner-friendly.

> **The senior manager is no longer confronted
> by the schematic entrails of the project**

But now we have arrived at the era of screen pictures of the subject of the project itself; very manager-friendly and customer-friendly. QEI contains all the standard features of traditional project planning software, but the detailed logic, often of mind-blowing complexity, put together by teams of discipline specialists, is concealed within pictures of the project itself. A senior manager is no longer confronted by the schematic entrails of the project, as described in this book. Instead he follows progress by means of a pictorial representation of project deliverables in terms with which he is familiar and comfortable. If the project is a ship he sees a picture of the ship, colour-coded as to degrees of completion throughout. To drill down to detail of the bridge, bulwarks or boiler room he merely clicks on a hot spot at the location in question and out pops the PERT chart, colour-coded in the standard way, or any other piece of detail he needs. In practice, of course, he leans back in his chair while the project manager does the clicking and explains the significance of the revealed detail. And the clicking can go down to whatever detail the discussion calls for.

QEI's graphical feature is a powerful CAD (Computer-Aided Design) program, enabling virtually any portrayal of a project to be connected to the planning details. The result needs to be seen to be believed, and is something I had been waiting for for some twenty years, fearing for several reasons that it would never happen. But to give you the full impact of the total system it is necessary to describe in a bit more detail the corporate system. It is a master class in how a modern company should be run, and serves as a model that I think many will be following as the ideas spread.

The AW Corporate Model

Because AW is essentially a project organisation it has made corporate sense to integrate everything possible into a single, all-pervading information system. At AW project planning is corporate planning. There isn't anything else at corporate level.

The choice of all-pervading system was determined by the corporate decision to make the Sales and Operations Planning system, SOP, the starting point, as opposed to the traditional hotchpotch of corporate systems: facilities management, financial systems, project planning or whatever, following Oliver Wight's dictum, "Forecasting is not simply a projection of future business but a request for resources to ensure the supply of a product". In principle you can start where you like, adding features as needed. And where you do so depends to a large extent on the current state of the computing art in the company, who in the company is doing what and with what combinations of hardware and software, many of which turn out in the long run to be blind alleys. But AW's decision was not only a wise one, it was a lucky one in that they selected a particular piece of software that made it easy to expand and embrace all the components of the corporation: bill of materials, human resources, both employed and contracted, physical resources, plant and machinery and work in progress. The entire edifice is called the Integrated Operational Support, IOS.

To this is added the firm order book and current programme plans, followed by internal statistically predictable factors such as spares and repairs, and finally the macro, binary, consequences of obtaining major contracts. This high-level study produces the following managerial indicators:-

> ***The aggregated workload:*** a histogram showing recent history, firm orders, anticipated orders and potential orders, all colour-coded and easy to understand by top management.
>
> ***Sensitivity charts:*** bar charts and histograms showing the results of loading the resource availability in response to changes in the initiation of projects; alarming increases in requirement from innocuous changes in start date.
>
> ***Project plan:*** top-level strategic view.
>
> ***Multiple resources:*** Operations, Customer Support, Engineering and Programmes.
>
> ***The SOP process:*** monthly budget against detailed planning.

These pictures provoke debate about assumptions not numbers. (Back in the 1950s Richard Hamming's mantra was, 'The purpose of computing is insight not numbers', even though he was an eminent numerical analyst and data integrity guru. I'd like to have seen the word ultimate in there somewhere because Hamming wasn't averse to getting a pay cheque produced by a computer, but he was indubitably right, and it has now all come to pass.) The result of all this is that at the board meetings the monthly ceremonies have been replaced by conversations, their slogan being, 'How do I know what I think until I can see what I say?' It's all about instant visibility.

Unifying the data

This terse description doesn't do justice to the wealth of data contained in the system, but it is vast, and only in recent times has it been possible to contain it all within the confines of a single computer system; combinatorial computing to the nth degree! But containing it in a computer is one thing, displaying it in digestible form is very much another. There is no point in amalgamating data if you can't use it. Moreover, if you are able to display it it needs to be instant, which is why the month's delay in transcribing data from Microsoft Project to Excel was unacceptable. It was all too tantalising. Tell me more. What if that anticipated contract date were to slip six months, what effect would it have on our resource loading? And tell me now. I need to know that to do my job. Data plus processing equals information. However, data plus processing plus graphics plus speed plus a device for all to see produces management information. Management is a team phenomenon; it needs all its members looking at a single picture at a point in time, and to be able to change the picture in answer to questions.

> **Data plus processing plus graphics plus speed plus a device for all to see produces**
> **– *Management Information***

Management is all about asking questions, the right questions, and effective management is all about getting answers fairly close to reality – and to getting them instantly. That's what AW's system does, and only today has that become possible. We are at a historical milestone in the history of computing and in the history of management, an apotheosis of the two. Only now can we claim in all honesty that the computer is a managerial tool. Switch off the boardroom whiteboard at AW and listen to the corporate howls. When the computer has become an indispensable part of corporate management it has finally arrived. This is very much a MIDAS, a Management Information, Decision and Action System, the result of combining data, calendars, logic, graphics and people into a single entity, with applications far beyond its function at AW. There's gold in them there meetings.

But to experience the thrill of it yourself visit PCF's website to see a demonstration of AW's interactive boardroom bar chart-histogram system. Or better still, take a trip down to Yeovil.

Simplicity reigns supreme

It must be fairly obvious to the reader that IOS has become a corporate catalyst, as indeed most computer applications have been throughout the evolution of computers, starting in Britain with the Leo machines of the 1950s. At AW:-

> Multiple distinctions are accepted as part of a robust organisation.
> Managers have come to rely on the monthly meetings as now an indispensable tool.
> People from different departments see their own data in a single **SOP** format.
> All conversation is in a common language, a little bit different perhaps to the disparate languages of the individual departments, and above all simplicity reigns supreme.
> Using versions of the system with the customer enables AW to:-
>> justify charging rates to the customers,
>> demonstrate the implications for procurement strategy,
>> explain their business strategy.
> And in discussions with the supply network AW is able to demonstrate capacity planning and commodity forecasting.

During the evolution of the system it was found that about 95% of the results were more or less as expected. But some 5% of the results produced otherwise surprising effects, even dire warnings not otherwise obtainable. These more than justified the process and hooked the managing director to the extent that he is quoted as saying during one of the budget rounds: "That is not what it says in the SOP model". That did it. The data came flooding in. The system has at its heart an accessible database enabling conversations that enhance decision making that justify the maintenance of an expensive accessible database; a neat circular argument.

And all encompassed within an instantly-available pictorial portrayal, the value of which has become the value of the company, justifying its cost by orders of magnitude.

The Computer as a Corporate Catalyst

As a postscript to this chapter, a story about the computer as a valuable catalyst. In the early days of computing, Marks and Spencer bought a machine and tried to program it to carry out what became eventually the usual universal commercial functions. However, they made the amazing discovery that the data from the shops came to headquarters in a jungle of varieties. You can't program chaos, so the computer stood there empty and unused for about a year while the company got its house in order. I suppose that must be the unique example of the infinite value of an unused computer.

The next chapter ...

... is about computer projects. What makes them different to traditional projects is that they are invisible; the boss can't see what's going on. A potted history of software development. Reliability, team size, maintenance, languages, current horror stories, lawyers.

Chapter 19: Computer Projects

A modern computer hovers between the obsolescent and the nonexistent

Sydney Brenner

The Invisibility of Computer Software

This chapter is of general interest. Everyone is invited to participate to consider why corporate computing is so expensive. The material of this book applies to all kinds of projects. It doesn't differentiate between one type and another: opera houses, highways, bridges, schools, theatricals or computer systems. The details differ greatly of course, but the principles are all the same. All projects need good planning, good follow-up whilst the work is being done, good colleague relationships, good documentation, etc. At the top level, they all have a common format using a common project language.

However, beneath the surface there is a wide crevasse between computer and other projects. Computer projects do not have anything equivalent to the bricks, mortar, pipes, wires, cranes or diggers of the visible project world. True, they have plastic or metal boxes containing electronics, but looking at them doesn't tell you very much. In the old days we housed our computers (which were very large) on raised floors in air-conditioned rooms with large windows through which the public incomprehensively stared. But today there's a computer on every desk coupled to the office computer sitting on the back of the moon. A myriad of different things can be going on inside these networks at virtually the same time, but you can't see what they are. Computer projects have an essential invisibility that separates them from all other projects, the invisibility of software. Computers don't even have the visibility of the paper they are supposed to eliminate.

**Computers don't have the visibility of
the paper they are supposed to eliminate**

Because of their invisible or concealed nature, software projects have to be handled differently. Good management practices are certainly essential but they are far from sufficient. Consider a manufacturing project. Design engineers, production engineers, etc all have thick handbooks on how to do things: international standards, legal requirements, etc. and there may be other restrictions such as standardised modules or particular parts that have to be employed. They may be limited by the laws of physics, preventing you doing just anything that happens to come to mind.

However, these restrictions do not exist in the computer world.

> **There is nothing so free in the industrial
> world as someone writing computer code**

The only "natural" limitation is the syntax of the programming languages that enable the bewildering panoply of today's computer devices to work. Good practices have evolved but unless programmers are strictly controlled, there is little to prevent badly structured programs, spaghetti code, twisted logic, etc.

In fact, there is nothing so free in the industrial world as someone writing computer code. There have been brave attempts to analyse this on the basis of Information Theory, whatever that may be. Another important difference is that a computer project is deemed essentially complete when it reaches the stage analogous to the detailed design in traditional projects; there is nothing equivalent to the production phase, the mixing of cement and the banging of metal, except for the hazardous business of plugging it all together.

Software Project Management

Software project management is far from being a trivial function. There are many books on the subject, but it isn't obvious that anyone reads them. The ultimate question you ask a programmer is, have you finished yet? The honest answer to which is always, no. The standard method of managing anything was invented independently by the Duke of Wellington and Thomas Jefferson. Their tools of the trade were the horse and telescope. The Duke's method was, armed with his telescope, to gallop at high speed in the hours before the battle to check on each individual position. He could see at a glance whether battle stations were as he had ordained. Up early and get there quickly. He didn't even have to ask. In the case of Thomas Jefferson, during the construction of the University of Virginia down in the valley below his villa, Montecello, he would watch everything through his telescope. He was his own architect and knew precisely what was supposed to be done each day. At every deviation from the design intent, he would mount his horse and gallop down to berate the offending bricklayer before the cement had had time to dry.

But horse-and-telescope management was easy. It was all patently visible. Not so computer software. The essential irony of modern civilisation is the fact that despite the polychromatic appearance of the computer screen, camera screen, telephone screen, in all their glory, the soft technology that makes it all possible is in itself utterly invisible. Have you finished yet? is an impossible question to answer because nobody knows. Only the true test of time will tell – despite the well-planned pre-release Greek-lettered testing that takes so much time, costs so much and is such a source of frustration to senior managers, people of limited sympathy. You can't think of everything – especially when trying to second-guess the myriad combinations of computer program states.

Computer programming is a combinatorial problem of unimaginable magnitude and incomprehension, comparable only to that of the square root of minus one.

> ## But horse-and-telescope management was easy

The Historical Perspective

As another approach to explaining why things are the way they are it is useful to consider the history of computer development. The first two, stored program, electronic digital computers began to operate in 1947 and 1948, at the Universities of Manchester and Cambridge respectively. Each of them occupied a lot of space compared to today's machines. But on the other hand each contained only a single K of memory: 1,024 words – or in today's parlance, bytes – each of some seventeen bits. In today's terms, their memories occupied only a small fraction of the head of a pin. And since the memory had to contain all there was of program and data – there was no such thing yet as a disk or tape of any sort – each was restricted to about five hundred words. Thus there was no possibility yet of handling data of any magnitude. All you could do was arithmetic: addition, subtraction, multiplication and division. You could sort a list of about a couple of hundred numbers into ascending or descending order, but you couldn't handle sentences, thus there was no possibility of using them to write letters. The irony of the first computers was that they were only capable of doing complicated (mathematical) things. As time went on and computers themselves got more complicated they became steadily better at handling simple things.

While the first machines could only handle numbers, this didn't stop their being put to substantial use. Indeed, the Cambridge machine, the EDSAC (the Electronic Delay-Storage Automatic Calculator) quickly became a service to the university. Any problem that could be expressed in numerical terms was a potential candidate for computer solution. Indeed some very sophisticated routines for performing integration and solving differential equations were written and placed in a program library for all to use – accompanied by documentation![26]

Since the first computer memories were so small, the first applications were strictly numerical problem solving, as opposed to data handling. Moreover, the first programmers were either mathematicians or physicists, or perhaps mathematically-minded engineers. Furthermore, there were very few of them, and each had his special interest at heart. Consequently, programs were written by individuals and not by teams, and took probably only a week or two to write. Or perhaps more accurately, a finished program was the result of an evolutionary series of mini projects; you grew programs as the ideas presented themselves. That isn't to say we didn't discuss what we were doing. At the Cambridge University Mathematical Laboratory, tea breaks were certainly a vital part of the early history of computing at Cambridge. In my case, to save paper I did my programming on the blackboard and anyone who felt like leaning on the doorway was most welcome to find my bugs. Indeed, it wasn't really true to say that computer programs were the result of formal projects as depicted in this book. No one gave us contracts. There was no such thing as a time or cost estimate. On the other hand, it was great fun solving other people's problems for them. We learnt a lot from it and steadily discovered how computers should really be designed; the evolution of computers has all the time been a series of solutions to computer problems, catalysed by solving non-computer problems.

The Computer Industry

Very shortly after the first two computers were up and running there emerged the advent of the computer industry. At first a purely hardware industry, with just enough software to make it usable by the customer, sprang up. That was in 1950. By 1960 already, American industry, commerce and government were locked into the use of computers, and the typical memory size was by now some 120K bytes, backed by miles of magnetic tape. This was a technical revolution of unprecedented as well as unpredicted

---

[26] It was some of the best computer documentation ever written, since when the standard has gone sadly downhill.

proportions. The rate of increase was still probably exponential, and the rest of the world was slowly awakening to what was going on.

By this time the requirement for harnessing computers to using organisations, in addition to the money, was the need for top quality programming teams working in well-organised project frameworks. If the short-lived university era was characterised by the happy-go-lucky programming described above, the commercial era was hemmed in by the twin pressures of delivery contracts and the urgency of getting the new systems going to aid the using organisation in an increasingly competitive world.

Data versus Numbers

Above all, what characterised the commercial computer most was its ability to handle data. The steady increase in computing capacity was important, but the advent of magnetic tape, 2,400 feet long at some 800 characters to the inch, housed in perhaps a dozen units per machine, was the essential breakthrough. By 1960 computers had become magnetic tape shunters. There was plenty of excitement in the computer rooms of old. Reels of magnetic tape oscillating backwards and forwards, sometimes even in opposite directions, secreted pints of adrenaline in the bodies of the computer operators, turning them grey before their time. Engineers quickly made use of the computers at their disposal, but it was the finance and manufacturing departments that made use of the sudden expansion of data-handling capacity; they had already had punched card installations for years, and switching to computers was a relatively easy and natural conversion. Furthermore, because much of the processing was concerned with the company's money, the programs had to work reliably. Thus, the implementation of computer systems had to be a process of almost unprecedented reliability. But the catalytic effect of the jump in magnitude of the data was reflected in the jump in the size of the teams of programmers required to make it all possible.

The one-man mathematical programming team became the five-man data processing team. And then we saw the evolving computer technology, initially hardware but followed quickly by some very necessary software, transferred to the factory. And lo and behold, the factory started to rely on the computer to do its job properly. Think of it, in 1950 we had hardly any computers at all but by 1960 they had become an inextricable part of the ways things were done in many of the world's largest manufacturing companies. The Boeing computers were cutting out aluminium parts by 1957 and drawing engineering lines by the early 1960s as we invented

CAD (Computer-Aided Design) on the 727 aeroplane. In 1950 absolutely no one (apart from me) cared whether or not my programs worked, but by 1960 if the daily factory instructions weren't delivered on time our lives were in jeopardy.

The Emergence of Reliability

The 1950s will eventually be recognised as the most revolutionary decade in the history of technology; industry and commerce went from not having ever heard of a computer to relying on them to get the job done. And a key part of that job was specifying and implementing the individual systems to run on this brand new equipment. In terms of the numbers involved, it took a team of five people to do the programming, but what was the system required to do? Someone had to decide. So the three-man specification team sprang up. That cost money and took time. And the system had to be tested, so up sprang the three-man Quality Assurance team who sometimes took more time to check it out than it took to create it in the first place. When it had settled down someone had to create the documentation: how to use it, how to report errors, how to submit methods of improving it and so on. "Improving it?" Ah, **Old Norman's Asymptotic Certainty Principle**, you don't really know what you want until you find yourself with something that you don't want. But the programmers created precisely what the specifications called for, as they interpreted them. Agreed, but the Specifiers are only human; they do not posses the gift of prophesy, any more than the creator of the first dinosaur. Most ideas sound good at the time.

> **You don't really know what you want until you find yourself with something that you don't want**

Leading on to Team Size

Adding all these mini-teams up now gives us something like fifteen people – not forgetting the manager. The size of a typical project team of that time was about one person per 2K of computer memory. We felt in those days that the memory size and project team size were comfortable. They were well matched. We could handle them. The natural composition of the team made for small groups. They could sit in a contiguous office area. They could easily interrupt one another to discuss a point of ambiguity, of which there were many. The team leader could easily know where the critical path lay. Little need for interminable meetings.

The Agony of Maintenance

In all the component parts of the project team in the early years, the need for continued work on the components of the programs was perhaps the least recognised, but in the long run it has become the major one; we call it maintenance.

Should he join the next project as Team Veteran?

The need for error fixing was well understood, and clearly the best people to fix bugs were their perpetrators. But this led to the problem of what was the best thing for a programmer to do when his current job seemed to be finished? Should he join the next project as Team Veteran to help them seek the profitability of a new system? By now he's had a whole year's experience. Or should he stay where he is for a while to squeeze more profitability out of the neophytic system and make it work properly? That was always the question, and people would get stuck with the continued development of a single system. It became their career and they would have to quit the company to get rid of it. This problem is still with us today.

The Emergence of Languages

Computer memory sizes stayed quiescent at around 30K to 50K for the period 1955 to 1965, and we built up a fairly good understanding of how to create projects of about that size. During that time of relatively peaceful hardware stability, we developed some rather good software. The problem was that the manufacturers were building computers (remember, at that time they weighed tons and had to be installed on a reinforced raised floor) faster than we could fill them with work. We needed some way of speeding up the business of programming. At the very start, we programmed very close to the level of the binary code designed into the hardware. We needed to lift ourselves up closer to the language of the application; the conversion of the description of a process from natural language to machine language had to be made much more efficient. This process started in 1957 with the programming language FORTRAN (Formula Translator) and has continued to this day, but all the time the speed and cheapness of the raw hardware has continued to outstrip that of the software.

Computer Hardware Disappears

Nevertheless, computer projects of the 1960s era were reasonably well run. But after about 1970, with micro-circuitry replacing traditional solid state, hardware prices began to tumble; costs had switched from hardware to software and by 1980 hardware became cheap and small enough for Woolworths to sell it. The cost of implementing computers became essentially the cost of implementing user projects. Consultants and computer salesmen were able to convince company management to mount more and more sophisticated systems based on more and more ingenious methods of connecting computers to fancy equipment.

But what has happened? Here cometh the denouement of this chapter. As I write (early, 2010) there are three major British system catastrophes, amongst others, on the go. They are described in more detail in the last chapter and are as follows:-

- The Fire Control System
- The Rural Payments Agency System
- The NHS Clinical Records System

Not All Government Projects are Disasters

Having said all that, I don't want to give the impression that all government computer projects are disasters. There are many successes. The income tax system works, sorry to say. The DVLA system erroneously told me a couple of years ago that I hadn't insured my car. However, it does now seem to work. The voting system seems to work, and there is also a myriad of systems within the NHS that work. Then what is it that makes some government systems failures?

Not All Commercial Ones are Successes Either; Far From It.

However, I don't want to give the impression either that the only successes are those of private companies. The difference is that private companies are able to keep their failures under wraps, whereas government failures invite the oxygen of publication in *Private Eye*. Efforts are made from time to time, in particular by the Standish group in Boston, to collect and publish data on computer system development. However, there is little incentive for private companies to admit their problems publicly – especially software companies, who need to look good to the potential customer. Nevertheless, published data show that some 30% of started projects do not reach completion; over 50% of projects cost around double their original estimates, and projects have reached completion containing as little as 40% of their original specification.

How can it be that a by now mature industry can fail so often to honour its contracts and deliver the goods? Well, it isn't alone in this respect. Non-computer projects also run into trouble. As I write, the British government is having trouble, for example, with some of its military projects. Large ones. Typically aircraft carriers – all apparently highly visible and manageable. On the other hand, as big as they are, aircraft carriers contain a lot of invisibility – much of it computer-related, as does your car.

Pull Harder! We are getting there!

The Infinity of Data

I think the main clue to the computer problem can be seen in the incomparable explosion in data volumes during the sixty years of the digital era. Going from the initial 1K to the typical 50K during the first decade or so was in itself a literally explosive growth. Canals, railways, motor cars, aircraft, etc had nothing on computers for growth figures. But we managed it and produced some very useful applications, not least in the industrial sector. Computers quickly became inextricably central to the business of building the things around us. It started with aircraft in the 1950s and quickly spread to everything to do with engineering. Had this not happened, the money that fuels today's computer industry would not have been there. The seeming infinity of data capacity is clearly very attractive to organisations that try to tame the seeming infinity of information they generate; not least hospitals. And the corresponding opportunity for consultants and software companies to come to their rescue is irresistible.

Fundamentally, there must be correlations between the magnitude of the data consumed by a computer system and the difficulty, elapsed time and cost of creating it – not forgetting the size of the project team. Obviously, the relationship cannot be linear, otherwise there wouldn't be enough people on this planet to do the programming. Perhaps the project size is proportional to the tenth root of the data size. There are of course nuances to this. There is a big difference between narrow and broad systems; between systems in which a repetitive simple action is taken on a high-speed series of similar numbers and on the other hand systems comprising a wide variety of different actions. It isn't a simple matter of adding up the data; it needs some form of characterisation and analysis.

And the Finiteness of Competence

However, whatever the truth of the matter, computer software companies can be very big. Nevertheless, it is doubtful whether there are indeed enough people of sufficient calibre to make all their projects successes. There is a vast difference between the best programmers and the average, but programming is an activity in which only the best are good enough. A fact that I cannot prove is that very few people make good computer programmers. But there's no reason why they should. Another unprovable fact is that women make better programmers than men. Unfortunately, all too few women seem to want to try their hand at it. A great opportunity awaits!

And Beware the Lawyers!

It is another unprovable fact that the computing companies' lawyers are cleverer than their programmers. They have to be. By an order of magnitude. To man up a large programming project you are forced to use people other than the best; they are bound to make mistakes and are bound in the process to sabotage contracts. This means that computer system contracts are bound to be fiercely defensive. If you are buying a computer system from another company your only defence is to hire even cleverer lawyers – or to ask me to help you. Reports concerning the current batch of disasters say that the costs of cancelling far outweigh the costs of continuing with the contract. Your fundamental defence is the baseline version of the project plan right there in the contract, as discussed in Chapter 6. Any departure from that and the contract is null and void. It's so easy. But did our erstwhile Prime Minister, himself a lawyer, pay any attention to a plan? Read the next chapter of this book and see what you think.

The next chapter ...

... surveys the spectrum of computer systems that essentially run this planet. Each one of these systems is the result of a project, and very many of them were quite cheap to make and work well – though they may need some simplifying. But at the centre of it all there are some very large, expensive systems under attempted development, each of which is a sorry lesson to us all.

Chapter 20: A Range of Projects

Go and look behind the ranges

Rudyard Kipling

Introduction

As with all professions and industries, there can be a very wide range of quality of the work done. Buildings and bridges fall down, water pipes leak, oil refineries catch fire. T'were ever thus and will continue to be. And this is with the very visible examples of projects. With invisible projects, such as computing, it is inevitably worse: there is and always be, an ever wider range of successful outcomes as hardware and software become ever more complicated and difficult to monitor. This final section of the book is concerned with computer systems that abound today in the business world, both the interaction between the general public and the organisations with which they interact.

Section 1: The peripheral Customer-Supplier Interface

Already in my book, *The Corporate Computer*,[27] from forty years ago, I said that the human mind was unable to evolve sufficiently to cope with the rapidly increasing quantity of information that the twentieth century world was creating. That, instead, the function of the computer was to trap this information and reduce it to a form manageable by people generally and by managers in particular. What I wrote was eminently true even in the 1970s, but it is vastly truer today than the most optimistic of us then could possibly have envisaged. Much has happened in the meantime, and we have reached the point now where if by some mischance all the computers in the world were to collapse we would all die – of hunger mostly. All the aircraft would fall out of the sky, all modern cars on the highway would crash, no telephones would work, no e-mail, no twitter, the shops would run out of food in hours and would stay empty. The Doomsday of all doomsdays!

---

[27] Published by McGraw-Hill (1973).

The reason for saying this is that it emphasises the fact that all the world is run by the computer – except perhaps on remote islands, where the people live on local fish. But, say what you like about computers, at the end of the day they work; they do what we instruct them to do. The customer interface sells tickets, it enables you to move money around, it accepts your orders to make deliveries, it issues your driving licence, it computes your tax return – and above all it tells you things – as long as you know how to ask the questions. It works. Indeed it works so well that if you don't happen to have a computer, or know how to use it, it even stops you doing things, such as buying tickets for the 2012 Olympic games.

It works. And if all development of the systems that constitute the interface, each of which is a project in its own right, remember, were to cease forthwith it would continue to work. But would it work well? What is the myriad of interface projects doing to improve the way the interface works? Are you, a bank customer, ticket purchaser or hotel booker, happy with it? Do you find it easy to use? Does your bank require you to know what a tab is? Do you get irritated at the whimsical changes foisted on the interface by the computer people behind it? Do your suppliers ever explain why they change things? Do your suppliers ever ask you for your opinion on the ease of use, the responsiveness, the transparency, etc of their systems? Indeed, do they ever invite you to contribute to their design? Indeed, who are the designers? The programmers? The Accounts department? The Sales department? The consultants?

My view, for what it's worth, of the quality of the computer system that runs this planet, is that it might have made a reasonable first stab at the job, but it has a long way to go. But it won't go anywhere if its perpetrators don't start involving their hoped-for customers. I know of only one system that goes anywhere near to satisfying my requirements for satisfaction, Traktor.com. Their home page consists of a short message, stuck up in the top left hand corner, telling you that "TRAKTOR is a group of filmmakers. We make films, not websites. Some of these films can be viewed below. If you are curious you can contact us here". This is followed by six entries to choose from. All in easy-to-see black lettering on a white background. No dancing dervishes. No advertising. No music. In short, no polychromatic unsolicited information to divert the attention. And each entry produces an equally simple list of possibilities from which to choose.

But even more to the point, the home pages of the global websites don't contain instructions for their use. You have to weave your eyes amongst a visual inferno of hotspots in an often hopeless quest to find your way to what you want. From the home page there should be a series of binary questions starting with – Are you a customer? Yes or no? If yes, the service department's routine takes over. This immediately gets rid of all the advertising and invites you to identify yourself. If no, you get the advertising routine. If yes, the system could then ask you another binary question such as, do you know exactly what you want? Yes should get you to the sales brochure in some way, while no could get you to a series of pictures, say, of generic options for sale by the company. And so on.

Of all of this, to my mind the worst thing these people do is make changes to systems that you've got used to. You've found out how to use a banking system. You've used it fluently for five years but then one Monday morning you find that what was green has gone blue, that there's a little cartoon animal laughing at you at the top left hand corner of the screen, there's no longer any way of getting into your account and they've removed the Contact Us telephone number. All this is a clear indication that a new project owner, intent on making his mark, has been hired.

That's probably all we need say about the Customer-Supplier Interface, the uncountable amalgam of smallish systems that enables the business world to function. But these are the least of our worries.

Section 2: The Central Stand-alone Systems

The interface systems tend to be fairly simple in design and have the advantage of being used thousands of times every day, enjoying plenty of quality control. Most of them are easy to write and are rarely objects of much public concern; they rarely appear in *Private Eye*. However, hidden more deeply behind the customer interface lie systems that can be very time-consuming and expensive to implement and install, and difficult to satisfy quality control tests. They are often the result of poor project management, leading to unwelcome publicity – again, often in *Private Eye*. Two relatively modest examples of this are the Fire Control System and the Rural Payments Agency System

The Fire Control System: The purpose of the system is to make it possible to unify the separate physical fire departments into a single logical entity, thereby maximising response to emergencies. As reported by the BBC, the original system was due to become operational in 2002 at a cost of £120 million. The goal is now to have it ready by 2013 at a cost of £423 million. The stated reasons for the delay and over-run are that there was insufficient detail in the specification and that the technical solution did not match what little specification there was. Delivery has been further sabotaged by changing to a new contractor. Any experienced computer technologist would tell you that this system will never reach completion. The only problem is that it isn't easy to prove it, other than to let it all happen and then say, I told you so. But you won't get rich telling people you told them so. (The above became history even as I wrote. The system was in process of being abandoned in the autumn of 2010, though how much it cost to do so is difficult to ascertain.)

The Rural Payments Agency System: The European Union makes payments to the remaining 100,000 British farmers via the Agency, and this could have been done by writing cheques by hand. Instead of that the Agency commissioned a computer system which is unnecessarily too complex for the task. It makes incorrect payments; it makes them late and it causes lamentations amongst the farmers; a lot of effort on both sides has to go into getting each transaction correct. As reported by the BBC, the project team consists of some one hundred people, costing some £200,000 each per year, a total annual computer cost of £20 million. These two systems in themselves are bad enough examples of what's going on in the computer world, but far worse is the NHS Care Records system which started in 2002 and seems to be still far from finished, and still costing this country considerable amounts of money that we can't afford. The following section is a short version of what appeared in a Government website in 2007.

The NHS Care Records and National Data Spine System: This system saw the light of day in February, 2002. The basic idea is that if you were to break a leg in Newcastle, say, the doctors there would be able to get hold of your patient record, held in Penzance, effortlessly and almost immediately. The initial estimate of cost was £2 billion, and the system was to take 2.75 years to complete. Ten years later the system seems to be nowhere near being delivered, and current cost estimates are impossible to obtain, though suggestions in the media are in the £20 billion region. What caused all this to happen? Who allowed so much tax-payer money to be spent on such a disaster? How should this project have been conducted? The reasons why this project became such a disaster are all explained in terms of what this book is all about, but it is too late for anything to be done about it. The money has been irretrievably spent, though work continues. But it is included in the book as a warning. It could happen again. And it could happen to you, so read carefully:-

Project Initiation: The initiation of this project consisted of a meeting in 10, Downing Street in February, 2002. The Downing Street meeting was attended by senior Cabinet and government people and the NHS Director of Information, none of whom is known as having project implementation experience. Furthermore, there were no medical professionals present; no doctors, nurses or anyone with any professional competence; no one who understood what was wanted. The project did not receive either a name or a number, but all present agreed that the NHS could and should be radically transformed by IT, seemingly unaware that hospitals, doctors' surgeries, laboratories etc were already well equipped with computers. The computer had already become ubiquitous. Further, it was not made clear what "radically transformed" meant.

Project Owner: No project owner was named at the 2002 meeting; it was not made clear who was responsible to Parliament or the NHS for ensuring the successful life of the project. Furthermore, no project owner has subsequently been named. The system is a super tanker without a rudder.

Project Manager: Neither was a project manager named at the meeting, though it must be surmised that one of the assembled company would have appointed the manager shortly after the meeting.

Project Specification: Though lofty goals were bandied about at the meeting, no one was given the task of specifying them with any degree of precision.

Time Estimates: How long would the project take to deliver? One of the participants stated three years. However, this answer was unacceptable to Tony Blair, so it was reduced to two years and nine months. No explanation has been given for its unacceptability.

Cost Estimates: The initial cost estimate was some £2.3 billion. However, a "blueprint" for the project was produced some time later, and the cost estimate was more than doubled to £5 billion. A report was published later in 2002, but the cost estimate was removed. Right from the very beginning it has been very difficult to obtain official cost estimates, in the absence of which the media has published a series of grotesque estimates, none of which have been robustly attacked. One wonders why the reticence to publish precise figures. Could it be that no one actually knows?

A Project Plan: No project plan was in evidence at the 2002 meeting, and no reference to such has appeared in the press, though no doubt at some time in the ensuing ten years one has been produce, or possibly many.

A Baseline: Since no plan was produced during the initiation, there was no baseline either. Therefore, it is not known beyond Downing Street what the time and cost estimates were based on.

The Evolving History: In May, 2003, bids were invited to produce not one but five projects to be installed in five regional monopolies. Bidding companies were each issued with a 500-page draft specification, with a deadline of just five weeks for bids to do the work. It isn't clear who wrote the specification nor to what extent it came from a detailed plan. Was it written by health professionals – doctors, nurses, laboratory workers etc? But more to the point, the idea of turning an unclear project into five, possibly also unclear, projects is unprecedented. Would any attempt be made to integrate them at some time in the future? If not, how could the whole caboodle be regarded as a single national system?

Acceptance Testing, Training and Continued Evolution: It is not known to what extent the draft specification contained any reference to acceptance testing nor to arrangements for continued system development or evolution following acceptance. The installation of a new computer system inevitably causes problems amongst the affected staff. It is vital that the staff are fully trained before the system is installed and are made aware of the installation plan and that they will be involved in it.

Eventual System Deliveries: As a means of giving you an impression of the success of delivered systems, the following table shows the number planned and delivered as at February and March, 2007.

NHS Care Records and National Data Spine System Administration and Clinical Systems (2007): Planned vs. Installed

Region / Provider	Admin Systems		Clinical Systems	
	Planned	Installed	Planned	Installed
NW & W Midlands/ **Computer Sciences Corporation (CSC)**	45	10	40	0
East / **Accenture**	27	0	27	0
North East / **Accenture**	22	2	22	0
London / **BT**	24	1	23	0
South / **Fujitsu**	37	3	37	0
TOTAL	**155**	**16**	**149**	**0**

Source: The Parliamentary NHS Committee website

By this time it should have been patently obvious to everyone involved that the system, as envisaged, had failed and that no further money should be spent on it. It would have been so nice to have been able to ask the project owner where the money had come from and what had been done with it. Regrettably no committee or individual (other than I) has ever asked this question, but answer came there none.

In summary:

In fact very little solid information seems to have been made public about a system that has lasted ten years and is seemingly still far from finished. Work is presumably still continuing; consultants and their lawyers are still being paid, but the NHS doesn't seem to be proud enough of what they've achieve to stand up and tell us about it.

Subsequently, there have been reports in the media that the Government is admitting that the NHS system has been a failure. We shall see. Britain is in recession, and anybody who could stop spending amounts of money in the billions would be hailed a hero. But no one does so. If good project practices had been adopted right at the beginning none of this would have happened. Take care that such things like this don't happen in your company.[28]

---

28 *"NHS contractor hosts US junket for health staff." Sunday Times, 14th October 2012.* One of the information technology contractors bidding on a contract worth between £250 and £400 million to provide a patient administration system and electronic patient record system for seven London NHS trusts has hosted a four-day conference for a large number of NHS staff. This does not sound like a project initiation meeting. One hopes that another catastrophe can be averted, that a Baseline has been properly agreed upon and that there is an experienced project management team in place. However, this system sounds uncannily like the circa £20 billion one described in this chapter.

Appendices – The Managerial Checklists

These checklists, set out on the next pages, summarise the responsibilities of the project management team, and act as a guideline for what the project owner and manager should look for when reading the book.

In the final analysis, the two roles and their checklists are very similar.

THE PROJECT OWNER'S CHECKLIST

This is a checklist for project owners. It is indicative of the range of factors determining a project, but is not exhaustive.

THE PROJECT MANAGER'S CHECKLIST

The full project manager's check list is the essence of Chapter 7. However, this checklist is a version of the book for project managers who have no time to read or aren't that interested in the detail of the subject matter (but who might find themselves sucked into reading it anyway).

Start here and see how far you get. The list is indicative of the range of factors determining a project, but is not exhaustive.

The Project Owner's Checklist

The Project Owner (PO):
- To whom is he accountable?
  - Shareholders or the Electorate
- What are his responsibilities and authority?
  - To whom does he report?
- To what extent should he be in regular contact with the project manager?
- How much detail should the PO know about the project?
  - At a very minimum the Baseline
  - Periodic updates?

Who is the Project Manager (PM)?
- Does he have the relevant experience of managing projects?
- Are his responsibilities and authority clearly defined?
- Is his position in the organisation clearly defined?
- How does the PM know what the team are doing?

The Baseline: Is there one?
- What is its essential importance?
- Has everyone from the PM upwards read it?
- Do the PM and PO agree with it?

The Project Plan: Is the Contract included in the Project Plan?
- Which comes first, the Project Plan or the PM?
- Are there arrangements for changes in the plan during the project?
- To what extent is the PM authorised to change the plan?
- Are the customer tasks included?
- What standard reports will be produced, who gets them and when?

Contracts: Is the Project Plan contained in the Contract?
- Is it a customer contract or an internal contract?
- Does it include acceptance testing and further development?
- Does it include customer training?
- Is it fixed-price or open-ended? If the latter, who signs off the payments?

The Project Team: will it be appropriately staffed?
- Will it comprise the right specialities to meet the plan?
- Who supplies them; company departments or contractors?
- Where will it work?
- What authority does the PM have over the Project Team?

Periodic Reviews: Who has the authority to stop the Project?
- Who is responsible for monitoring the Actual vs. Budget expenditure?
- Have Periodic Review dates been identified in the Baseline?

The Project Manager's Checklist

Who is a Project Owner (PO) to whom the Project Manager (PM) reports?
- ▶ What are his responsibilities and authority?
- ▶ Where does he belong in the organisation?
- ▶ Where is his ultimate career destination?
- ▶ How much detail should the PO know about the project?

The Project Manager
- ▶ What are the PM's responsibilities and authority?
- ▶ Where does the PM fit into the organisation?
- ▶ To what extent is the PM allowed to plan the project?

Contracts: Is the contract contained in the plan?
- ▶ Is it a customer contract?
- ▶ Or an internal contract for carrying out company work?
- ▶ Is it fixed-price or open-ended?
- ▶ Does it include acceptance testing and further development?

The Project Plan: Is the plan contained in the contract?
- ▶ Are the customer tasks included?
- ▶ What are the arrangements for maintaining the plan during the project?
- ▶ What standard reports are required?

The Project Management Team
- ▶ How does the PM relate to the project management team?
- ▶ Where does the project management team come from?
- ▶ How many people and of what specialities are required?
- ▶ Who supplies them: company departments vs. contractors?
- ▶ Where will they work: home based vs. team area?
- ▶ How does the PM know what the team are doing?

Periodic Reviews
- ▶ Have Periodic Review dates been identified in the Baseline?
- ▶ If the project is likely to exceed the budget, is the PM aware of whom to inform?
- ▶ If the project becomes undeliverable, is the PM aware of whom to inform?

Glossary

Accounts Payable Pointer: (APP) a Task field listing all accounts payable documents.

Accounts Receivable Pointer: (ARP) a Task field listing all accounts receivable documents.

Actual Finish (AF): A Task field where one replaces the Planned with the Actual Finish date.

Actual Start (AS): task fields where one replaces the Planned with the Actual Start date.

AF: see Actual Finish

Analysis: the analysis of a network consists of computing the Earliest Start and Finish Times and Latest Start and Finish times of each Task. Analysis is based on time estimates and constraints only, ignoring the availability of other resources.

APP: see Accounts Payable Pointer.

ARP: see Accounts Register Pointer.

AS see Actual Start.

Asymptotic Certainty Principle - Old Norman's: "You don't really know what you want until you find yourself with something that you don't want."

Augusta Westland: the Anglo-Italian helicopter company owned by Italy's Finmeccanica, is a total capability provider in the vertical lift and helicopter markets.

AW: see Augusta Westland.

Babel-fish: from *The Hitchhiker's Guide to the Galaxy,* by Douglas Adams. The babel-fish, placed in the ear, automatically translates between any two languages. All project managers should be issued with one.

Backward Pass: a methodology in which the latest finish and start times for the tasks in a network are calculated.

Baseline Plan: the final version of a plan prior to a project going live; the version of the plan containing all the time and cost estimates that form the basis for the project contract.

Big Bong: the noise made by the project owner's gong at the moment a project goes live.

Brabazon: (1949), an attempt at building an aircraft for post-war civil traffic. It was aimed to be ahead of its time; far too large and expensive and many of its components were insufficiently tested; an unnecessarily long leap from the then tried and tested aircraft technology.

Breakdown Structure: a method of describing the structure of a machine, building etc, enabling estimates of costs and times required to build it to be made, as well as reporting against the estimate.

Budget Document: any document containing budget information; the interest in this book is that of creating it using a project planning system even when its use does not pertain to a project.

CEO: Chief Executive Officer.

Certainty Principle - Old Norman's: if you can see the one you can't see the other. This is an echo of Heisenberg's Uncertainty Principle in which if you know where a particle is you cannot know its velocity – and its supplementary, you cannot find the temperature of the bath water without changing it.

Come to God Meeting: a meeting held at the end of a project where the people involved discuss all the major mistakes made during the project to learn how to do it better next time.

Commitment Document: this is the Project Plan in the form of an internal contract. It is signed by all the department heads who will be required to provide resources to enable the project to be completed.

Company Organisation Chart: illustrates the inner structure and hierarchy within a company.

Constraint: see Relationship.

Criticality Report: a daily report which highlights all the Tasks in the project which are in danger of slowing the project down. It is a "what-to-do-right-now" report.

Critical Path: a series of Critical Tasks in a PERT chart; a delay in any one of them will cause a delay in the entire project.

Critical Task: a Task of zero Float.

Day Zero: the day the project starts; the day the Big Bong is rung.

Delphi operator: a member of the project team with the responsibility of creating unforeseen and unplanned reports.

Document Management System: (DMS) an electronically indexed document retrieval system, itemising the location of all the documents, plans, electronic files, e-mails, etc, which relate to the Project. It is of fundamental importance.

DMS: see Document Management System.

Documents Received: a file containing copies of all documents received by the project.

Document Register: a.k.a. Spine Document or Spine Register.

Drawing Register: (DR) an electronically indexed drawing retrieval system cataloguing the paper and electronic drawings relating to the Project.

Drawing Register Pointer: (DRP) a Task field containing the address of the Drawing Register.

Drill Down: a process of using a coding scheme on the computer screen to interrogate information detail at multiple layers of a project, at the behest of the user.

DRP: see Drawing Register Pointer.

DU: see Duration.

Duration: an estimate of the time a Task should take, or the time it took.

DVLA: Driver and Vehicle Licensing Agency.

Earliest Finish: the earliest date by which a Task can be completed.

Earliest Start: the earliest date at which a Task can be started.

Elephant Problem: something in which it is too big to see all the constituent parts.

EF: see Earliest Finish.

ES: see Earliest Start.

Feasibility study: a preliminary project appraisal, the purpose of which is to try to determine whether a project is viable.

Finish Times: the expected time when individual Tasks will be completed.

Float (Flt): the time difference between the earliest and latest starts of a Task; the amount of time a Task may be started after its Earliest Start without becoming critical.

Flt: see Float.

Forward Pass: a methodology whereby the earliest start and finish times for Tasks in a network are calculated.

Godot: *Waiting for Godot* is a play by Samuel Beckett in which two characters spend their time waiting for something to happen. It takes for ever to get documentation written, so the Godot subproject is a joke meaning that a substantial part of the time taken by a project consists of waiting for the documentation to arrive.

HCPS: see Holistic Corporate Project Service.

Hod Head: chief bricklayer. A hod is a V-shaped container used for carrying bricks.

Holistic Corporate Project Service: a Project/Programme Office with the complete responsibility for carrying out all corporate projects.

ID: as in ID1, ID2, ID3, ...the identifier of the individual tasks in a Project.

Information Container: a Task file containing ID references to all documents pertaining to a Project.

Information Theory: the mathematical analysis of the efficiency with which communication channels are employed.

Integrated Operational Support: embraces all the components of the company: bill of materials, human resources, both employed and contracted, physical resources, plant and machinery and work in progress.

IOS: see Integrated Operational Support.

Latest Finish: the latest date by which a Task can be completed.

Latest Start: the latest date at which a Task can be started.

Law of Computer Programming - Old Norman's: the best time to write a computer program is immediately you've successfully used it.

Law of Inverse Momentum - Old Norman's: the probability of stopping a non-starter is inversely proportional to how long ago it actually started.

Law of Learning - Old Norman's: the key to success in learning things in this life is to be fortunate enough to surround yourself with patient, friendly people who are willing to straighten you out.

Law of Project Planning - Old Norman's: the best time to make a plan is when you've successfully completed the project.

Lessons Learned Log: a diary of useful knowledge picked up from running projects.

LF: see Latest Finish.

Logic bar chart: a bar chart version of a PERT chart; the duration of a Task is represented by its length.

LS: see Latest Start.

Microsoft Project: one of the many Project Planning programs used by project managers to schedule the Activities and identify the Floats and Critical Paths.

MIDAS: a Management Information, Decision and Action System, from *A Manager's Guide to Profitable Computers*, (1978), Norman Sanders, published by Associated Business Programmes Ltd.

Milestones: points in time at which major events are due to occur.

Modus vivendi: a way of people working together with a minimum of disagreement.

MSP: see Microsoft Project.

Network analysis: the process of computing times and dates of Tasks arrayed in a PERT chart.

Network diagram: a means of displaying a PERT chart, each Task represented by a box, with the logic shown as lines joining the boxes.

Payment Round: points in a Project Plan at which payment for work done must be made.

PCF (PCF Ltd): A company whose software makes it possible to encase all the details of a project plan in a picture of the project itself.

Percent complete: a method of computing the degree to which a project has been completed, to provide the basis for part payments for work done on incomplete Tasks.

PERT: originally Polaris Evaluation Review Technique, now Project... A method of arranging project Tasks in a logical order, allowing the systematic evaluation of times and dates during the planning phase and while carrying out the Project.

Peter Principle: "In a hierarchy every employee tends to rise to his level of incompetence." Professor Laurence Peter pronounced this in his eponymous book, published in 1969. To "Peter out" is to reach that level.

PI: see Project Initiation.

Planner: a person who understands the details, including the eccentricities, of a software planning system and knows how to use them to plan a project.

Planning Document: a printed version of a Project Plan plus any associated documents.

Pointer: a table contained by a Task, containing references to each document within its purview, making it easy to locate.

Predecessor: a Task immediately before the Task in question.

PRG: see Project Review Group.

Primus inter pares: **first among equals,** describing the most senior person of a group sharing the same seniority in the organisation.

Process Breakdown Structure: a diagram which contains the times and costs of doing the work in a project.

Product Breakdown Structure: a diagram which contains such information as material codes, prices and weights for a project.

Programme Office: also known as the Project Office.

Progress Payments: payments for work carried out on a project before it has been accepted by the customer.

Project Assistant (Secretary): a person who reports to the project manager and looks after the daily details of the work being done in the context of the project Plan. The project housekeeper. This position is an excellent one for a fledging project manager to learn the trade.

Project Initiation: the process in which a project comes to life.

Project Manager: the daily leader of a project, responsible for the plan being carried out, reporting progress to the project owner.

Project Office: also known as Programme Office. Responsible for the management of the projects, the computer substrate, project time-sheets, data acquisition, training, etc. At the core of the corporate structure.

Project Owner: the person appointed by a company for being responsible for a project at top corporate level; responsible for securing the project budget; the face of the company to the project team and the face of the project to company management; the project champion.

Project Plan: a network of tasks to be carried out to implement a project.

Project Review Group: a group of company employees who meet regularly to discuss the requirements of a potential project from the original idea to the start of its implementation.

Project Team: the people who carry out the work of a project.

Project Organisation Chart: a chart, similar to a company organisation chart, displaying the names of the key people for the duration of a project.

Relationship: the condition connecting two or more consecutive Tasks in a PERT chart; examples, finish-to-start, finish-to-finish, start-to-start; constraint.

Remaining Duration: the current estimate of the time needed to complete a Task which has been started.

RESOx: as in RESO1, RESO2, RESO3, ... A resource field code which identifies a specific resource.

QEI: the Project Planning system of the PCF company.

Risk: the level of uncertainty of a Task or set of Tasks.

S-Curve: a display of cumulative costs, labour hours or other quantities, plotted against time. It is shaped like an S.

Scenario analysis: The process of estimating the impact on a project, after a given period of time, assuming specific changes in the key factors that will affect the project. Scenario analysis commonly focuses on estimating what the outcome will be of the "expected-case scenario" if all goes to plan; the "worst-case scenario" when specific items do not go to plan, and the "best-case scenario" when things go better than expected.

Schedule: the times and dates derived from the analysed dates after applying resource requirements. Resource-limited scheduling uses at most the amount of resource available, and times and dates may exceed the analysed times and dates; time-limited scheduling uses sufficient resources to maintain the analysed dates.

Sensitivity Analysis: this involves altering the key variables of the project one by one to assess the sensitivity of the project to each variable.

Simulation: A problem solving technique used to approximate the probability of certain outcomes, of the key variables in a project, by running multiple trial runs using random numbers for each of the key variables.

Slippage: the amount of float time used up due to a delayed start or increased duration.

SOP: Standard Operating Procedure. It details all the steps and activities of a process or procedure.

Spine Document: this is the document register which shows where all the documents relating to the project are located.

Spine Register: a.k.a. Spine Document or Document Register.

Spreading the Gospel Meeting: similar to the Come to God meeting, to which members of other company projects are invited to learn from its mistakes.

Start Times: the times at which individual Tasks are due to start or have started.

Successor: a Task immediately following the current Task.

Task: a unit of work; an almost indivisible component of a project; examples, dig trench, lay cable, cover trench, re-dig trench, lay water pipe, recover trench.

Task Information: details of a specific task within a project.

Task Manager: (TM) the person responsible for carrying out a Task – though he may not necessarily do the work.

Time Sheet Function: the recording of the actual hours spent on the Tasks of a Project.

TM: see Task Manager.

VO: see Variation Order(s).

Variation Order(s): change(s) to the plan during the life of a project, resulting from unpredicted problems that have been encountered.

VP: Vice President.

Warm bodies: people.

WBS: see Work Breakdown Structure.

Wittgenstein: one of the great philosophers of the twentieth century. His name is used in the book to symbolise the philosophical nature of the problem.

Work Breakdown Structure: a methodology used for defining the hierarchical structure of work required to deliver the products of a project. The major categories are split into smaller components. These are sub-divided into the smallest stand-alone components, generally known as work packages. The WBS defines the total work to be undertaken on the project and provides a structure for reporting costs and times spent on its major components.

Zero Float: a critical task that has no slack in its scheduling: if it is delayed it will cause the whole project to be delayed.

Index

Page numbers in bold show that the word or phrase is also in the Glossary.

Page numbers in bold show that the word or phrase is also in the Glossary.

The Project Manager is also available as an enhanced eBook.

Visit **www.eBooktumble.com** and discover more about this book, its author, and about other books and authors.

This book is available in the following eBook formats

ISBN: Kindle	9781906960605
ISBN: EPUB	9781906960612
ISBN: PDF	9781906960629

Galleons
Green

www.galleonsgreen.com

**Projects are best carried out far from home,
where there is nothing to do in the evenings or at the weekends**

Lightning Source UK Ltd.
Milton Keynes UK
UKOW040029280113

205427UK00008B/176/P